RETURN
TO AUTHENTIC
CHRISTIANITY

Books by Robert Stearns

Keepers of the Flame

Prepare the Way (Or Get Out of the Way!)

The Cry of Mordecai

Books by Chuck D. Pierce

One Thing

Releasing the Prophetic Destiny of a Nation

Books by Larry Kreider

Building Your Life on the Basic Truths of Christianity

Building Your Personal House of Prayer

Discovering the Basic Truths of Christianity

House to House

Supernatural Living

21 Tests of Effective Leadership

Available from Destiny Image Publishers

RETURN
<u>TO</u> AUTHENTIC
CHRISTIANITY

An In-depth Look at
12 Vital Issues Facing Today's Church

ROBERT STEARNS, CHUCK D. PIERCE,
LARRY KREIDER

DESTINY IMAGE® PUBLISHERS, INC.
P.O. Box 310, Shippensburg, PA 17257-0310

"Speaking to the Purposes of God for This Generation and for the Generations to Come."

This book and all other Destiny Image, Revival Press, MercyPlace, Fresh Bread, Destiny Image Fiction, and Treasure House books are available at Christian bookstores and distributors worldwide.

For a U.S. bookstore nearest you, call 1-800-722-6774.
For more information on foreign distributors, call 717-532-3040.
Reach us on the Internet: www.destinyimage.com.

Trade Paper ISBN 13: 978-0-7684-3134-6
Hardcover ISBN: 978-0-7684-3471-2
Large Print ISBN: 978-0-7684-3472-9
E-book ISBN: 978-0-7684-9105-0

For Worldwide Distribution, Printed in the U.S.A.
1 2 3 4 5 6 7 8 9 10 11 / 13 12 11 10

Dedication

We dedicate this book to the Lord and to the faithful servants of Christ in our generation who are focused on listening to and obeying the voice of God in our day.

Acknowledgments

A special thanks to Karen Ruiz, editor and writing assistant who helped gather and organize the material for this book. Also thanks to Peter Bunton, Brian Kooiman, and Sarah Wolf for their valuable input.

Table of Contents

Introduction

It was the best of times, it was the worst of times,
it was the age of wisdom, it was the age of foolishness,
it was the epoch of belief, it was the epoch of incredulity,...
it was the spring of hope, it was the winter of despair....
—Charles Dickens

That's how Dickens began his book, *A Tale of Two Cities*. It could also describe the reality of today's Church with its sometimes contrasting and contradictory trends, twists, and turns.

Among the three of us authors, our combined mileage in travel is more than half a million miles each year. Wherever we go, we see current trends in the Body of Christ that impact us. Some of the trends we see today are positive and some are alarming.

In some ways, it's a challenge to minister in times like these. We see Church leaders who are faltering, sometimes through a lack of integrity or by failing to pass the baton to younger leaders. Some say American churches are watering down the Gospel in order to attract crowds. The younger generation shows a diminished interest in church attendance, yet is hungry for authentic Christianity. A lack of unity in the Church often reveals the good, the bad, and the ugly sides of church life. Still, some believe that while we are hearing a negative spin on what is happening in the Church, things really aren't as bad as statistics make them out to be.

But there are also very positive trends in parts of the Body of Christ. Some nations are experiencing incredible revival. God is turning the hearts of the fathers to their children and the hearts of the children to their fathers (see Mal. 4:6). God is pouring out great blessing in some places as His Church has come together in unity.

While troubling trends can produce fear, they also provide opportunities for change. That is what this book is about—taking a candid look at some trends in the Church and giving hope regarding how we can be authentic believers, accountable to one another, and a Church working together as we become agents of change in our world. Obviously these trends are not exhaustive; however, we think they are significant in reshaping and impacting the Church today.

In these best of times and worst of times we must be like the men of Issachar who understood the times and knew what they should do (see 1 Chron. 12:32). We can't solve all the problems, but we must begin to see how our actions impact future generations.

The worst of times can be "the best of times" for the Church to proclaim the good news of hope through God's Word as His Kingdom continues to expand. It is an opportunity to be "the salt of the earth" and "the light of the world" as we joyfully trust in Him and seek first His Kingdom (see Matt. 5:13-14; 6:33).

We trust that the Lord will give you great revelation and understanding of His purposes as you read each page.

Robert Stearns
Chuck D. Pierce
Larry Kreider

12 Vital Issues Facing Today's Church

- ～ The younger generation leaving church
- ～ The emergence of a "gray" Church
- ～ A hunger for the basics
- ～ Harassment of the Church
- ～ Controversy surrounding Israel
- ～ The redesigning of church
- ～ The changing complexion of church leadership
- ～ Recognition of modern-day apostles
- ～ The emergence of regional churches
- ～ The distinctions between traditional church and authentic discipleship
- ～ New intergenerational connections
- ～ The focus on marketplace ministry

Chapter 1

A New "Mindskin"

BY CHUCK D. PIERCE

‹‹‹‹‹‹‹‹‹‹‹‹‹‹‹‹‹‹‹‹‹‹‹‹‹‹‹

*Our "mindskin" produces God's
wineskin for today and our future!*

B uilt on revelation, the Church advances the Kingdom of God in the earth. We have entered a new
season in the history of the Church. Like each generation before us, we must have a structure that is relevant
to express Jesus Christ, our Messiah, in this present age.

The most critical issue for today is how we think. We
express every structure of society based upon our thought
processes. Those who connect their thoughts with God's
thoughts can change the history of the world in their age.

The Church as a whole is undergoing a major transition.
Like the children of Issachar, we must understand the times
in which we live so we can transition correctly (see 1 Chron.
12:32). Scholars and watchers of Church trends agree that God
is fashioning a new wineskin for His Church that will cause us
to arise and take a stand against the kingdom of darkness.

New Wine Is Pouring!

The transition taking place in the Body of Christ is really a changing of wineskins (see Mark 2:22). The new wine
God is longing to pour into His Body includes the power,

understanding, and wisdom that we will need to face the future war of the Church. Changing the wineskin—in this case a changing of government in the Body—is a crucial part of our preparation for the war.

In his book *The Complete Wineskin*, Harold R. Eberle writes:

> Whenever the Holy Spirit fills people with "new wine," the structure or organization in which they function must change. Old wineskins rip. New wineskins must be used to hold the additional life and power of God.... The time for God to move is at hand. Therefore, we should expect our present wineskins to rip.... There can be no mighty spiritual awakening in our day without a great shaking of our Church organizations, leaders, and structures. If you are looking for the Second Coming of Jesus, or if you are praying to God to move upon your church, your city, your local schools, your family, or your own heart, then the first thing you must look for is a new wineskin.[1]

The new wine only comes when it's time for God to give the Church revelation for how to be victorious in the next season. To do that, God has to restructure our wineskins in order to lay the foundations we need for future victory. Graham Cooke writes:

> There is a new prototype of church emerging that will clash with the world and institutional Christianity. A prototype is the first in a series. The Church will rediscover her radical edge, but not by playing with the world's toys and using them differently. Real radical behavior in church is grounded in the supernatural. It proceeds from

the mouth of God; it emanates from simple obedience to His ways; it emerges out of Holy Spirit boldness to follow the plans of God with fervent faith. It is to be willing to look foolish in order to confound the world.

We all will be pioneers in this next move of God. His plans for our churches will mean profound changes to the structure, vision, personality, and effectiveness of our meetings, missions, training, and discipleship forums. We will see a radical change in leadership style and methodology.

When building a prototype church, all our mistakes are public. One thing we should note here: Real pioneers do not criticize other pioneers because they know how hard it can be to build something new. Settlers usually make the most vicious of critics. They haven't done it themselves and have no intention of taking what they perceive to be insane risks. Their credo is that it is better to snipe from the sidelines and then borrow the new thing once it has been proved out. Some even argue that it is their "refining" comments that have played a valuable part in maturing the original concept.[2]

Let's take a look now at what this new wineskin will look like in the days ahead.

A New "Mindskin" for the New Wine!

In May 2009, we were having a gathering at Glory of Zion International Ministries. Jerry Tuma, a well-known business person who understands economic systems, was speaking on "How the Economy Will Continue to Shift."

When the time came for him to address the changes occurring in the economic community and the effects of those changes on the Church, he said, "So, to meet these changes head-on, we must have a new *mindskin!*"

Even though Jerry meant *wineskin*, I immediately got up from my seat and shared with the congregation that Jerry's slip of the tongue was really what a new wineskin is about—the way we think! Perhaps we need to allow a shift to occur in our thinking so we reflect the mind of God in the way we structure our ministries, businesses, families, and lives in the days ahead.

I would have to say that one of the keys to our future is the structure that is forming today. How we are thinking today does not just affect the belief system of our generation. Instead, it causes the next several generations to be influenced. I believe the most incredible challenge in the Body of Christ is to think the way the Lord thinks first, and then set our plans for the future.

In the coming chapters, let's begin to look at some of the current trends we see in the Body of Christ, and then ask the Lord how we should respond in times like these.

Endnotes

1. Harold R. Eberle, *The Complete Wineskin*, 4th ed. (Yakima, WA: Winepress Publishing, 1997), 1, 2.

2. Graham Cooke, *A Divine Confrontation* (Shippensburg, PA: Destiny Image Publishers, Inc., 1999), 285.

Chapter 2

A Younger Generation Is Leaving the Church

BY LARRY KREIDER

∽∾∽∾∽∾∽∾∽∾∽∾∽∾∽∾∽∾∽∾∽∾

*The younger generation feels
disengaged from church life.*

Young adults are leaving Christian churches in America in record numbers, according to several surveys in recent years. Some contend that we have an epidemic on our hands.

In the book *Already Gone: Why your kids will quit church and what you can do to stop it*, Ken Ham and Britt Beemer cite the following statistics from George Barna:

> Respected pollster George Barna was one of the first to put numbers to the epidemic. Based on interviews with 22,000 adults and over 2,000 teenagers in 25 separate surveys, Barna unquestionably quantified the seriousness of the situation: six out of ten 20-somethings who were involved in a church during their teen years are already gone. Despite strong levels of spiritual activity during the teen years, most twenty-somethings disengage from active participation in the Christian faith during their young adult years....[1]

Another survey by LifeWay Research revealed that "more than two-thirds of young adults who attend a Protestant church for at least a year in high school will stop attending church regularly for at least a year between the ages of 18 and 22."[2]

A considerable number spend more than a year away. Recurrent reasons for the temporary, if not permanent departure from the Church include lifestyle changes and frequent moving; pastoral disdain or disagreement; and political, ideological, and theological disagreement with Church positions.

In *Already Gone*, Ham unveils Beemer's startling statistics that show two-thirds of young people in evangelical churches will leave when they move into their twenties. One of the most challenging statistics in the survey revealed something they didn't expect:

> Most people assume that students are lost in college….but it turns out that only 11 percent of those who have left the Church did so during the college years. Almost 90 percent of them were lost in middle school and high school. By the time they got to college they were already gone! About 40 percent are leaving the Church during elementary and middle school years! Most people assumed that elementary and middle school is a fairly neutral environment where children toe the line and follow in the footsteps of their parents' spirituality. Not so. I believe that over half of these kids were lost before we got them into high school! Whatever diseases are fueling the epidemic of losing our young people, they are infecting our students much, much earlier than most assumed.[3]

This is sobering news for the Church. Why aren't our children gaining a solid Christian worldview? Why do they often grow into adulthood and not know what they believe?

Dr. R. Albert Mohler, Jr., president of the Southern Baptist Theological Seminary, says:

> [Our children's] worldview was evidently not shaped adequately by biblical truths such that they were able to withstand the tide of the secular culture and the allure of the other worldviews around them.... [Churches] promote the idea of the church as a full-service entertainment and activity center, where you take children away from their parents and just put them in a different peer culture. Now it's a church peer culture...and many of those activities have very little theological, biblical, or spiritual content. As a result, we have a generation of young people who believe that there is a God, but they don't have any particular god in mind.[*]

Parents cannot depend on the Church to train, educate, and nurture their children in the faith. They must engage their children in everyday life while confronting them with biblical truth and grounding them in the Scriptures. Too often, Bible accounts are presented as mere stories rather than meaningful biblical history.

It is a challenge for parents to instruct their children in such a way as to inspire a biblical worldview. Our youth have to be able to filter the information they receive through the biblical worldview they believe comes from an infinitely good, wise, and holy God.

Training like this can be accomplished in even ordinary ways. For example, after watching the nightly news or viewing a movie, parents should talk about the worldviews represented onscreen. They should ask their children questions, such as: Do these views conflict with a biblical worldview or reinforce it? What is God's standard and how does this particular presentation line up?

Both parents and the Church must do a better job of helping young people to integrate their faith with what they hear at school and in the surrounding culture.

Young People Want Authenticity

The statistics from the previously mentioned surveys show that the primary reason for leaving the Church is that the young generation finds their churches irrelevant to their lives. Often, they don't feel engaged or welcomed. A high percentage finds its members to be judgmental or hypocritical.

Today's young adults value authenticity. They witnessed a generation of baby-boomer Christians who required the appearance of excellence in every part of church life. The boomers' cultural trend of "image is everything" was reflected in their churches.

> Boomers proclaimed in the 1980s that image is everything, and their churches have reflected that cultural trend. The nurseries have got to be sparkling clean, the church buildings are marvelously functional…the Sunday services are seamless with perfect transitions (just like television), the preaching is entertaining and informative (but not so deep as to offend visitors), and the plants on stage are beautiful (but artificial).

As a result, according to Dieter Zander, the next generation has concluded that "everything is image," and therefore nothing can be trusted. Church is too slick, too good, too polished to be real. And the twenty-something hunger for raw authenticity just doesn't fit in.[5]

Young people today want reality. They don't want slick Christianity. They want to be honest about their struggles. They want leaders who admit to difficulties in following Christ and who give them hope that they can make mistakes and still keep following Jesus without judgment from others in the Church.

What They Look for When They Come Back

The good news is that many who leave do eventually return, according to LifeWay's research:

> Among church dropouts who are now ages 23-30, 35 percent currently attend church twice a month or more. Another 30 percent attend church more sporadically. Thus, about two-thirds of those who leave do return at some level.

> This return to church after being gone for at least a year is primarily the result of encouragement from others. The most common reason for returning is "My parents or family members encouraged me to attend" (39 percent). Twenty-one percent attribute their return to "My friends or acquaintances encouraged me to attend." Combined, 50 percent of those who return were influenced by the encouragement of either family or friends.[6]

We cannot help but notice that relationships are a large part of why church dropouts return. Young people want community; they want to be understood, accepted, respected, and included. They are searching for genuine experiences, especially those involving family and friends.

Sometimes when young people return they look for a new kind of church. Some embrace nontraditional house churches. They appeal to some young people because they offer the kind of casual and informal church experience to which they can more easily relate.

We need churches of all shapes and sizes and forms to come together to reach the world. These new kinds of churches very often fit the heart, call, and passion of the younger generations. *Religion Today* published an article that explains to some extent the appeal of house churches to the younger generation. Mostly, the appeal comes from the "relationship" context found in them.

> The generation of 18 to 35-year-olds, less concerned about structure and hierarchy, are disconnected from traditional churches and starting small, informal fellowships…. The churches meet in homes, coffee shops, warehouses, fast-food restaurants, industrial complexes, parks, and other unconventional places….[7]

Today's generation has a pervading culture that is all its own. There is no reason why the unlikely duo of traditional churches and house churches cannot work together and support one another. Indeed, some conventional churches are launching house churches and many are finding new ways to train people to lead a congregation or start a small group. I firmly believe house churches and conventional churches can learn from each other. None of us has it completely right.

> Mega Churches need to learn how to have community and care for people on a personal level better than they do. House Churches need to learn how to serve beyond the boundaries of their group and be part of a global church. Mega Churches can bring some of the best teaching, resources, and logistical support that we could ever hope for as we work to serve the King. House Churches bring a nimbleness, an openness to the move of the Spirit that allows us to see and hear what God is doing that might not fit our strategic plan.[8]

If the Church hopes to reconnect with young people and others who have disconnected from the Church, we will have to be honest about the shortcomings of the Church and identify our role in them. Christians must be transparent and humble as they willingly talk about their beliefs with those who are disenfranchised or have questions. As First Peter 3:15 advises: *"Always be prepared to give an answer to everyone who asks you to give the reason for the hope that you have. But do this with gentleness and respect..."* (NIV).

Young people respond to those who are real. They yearn for transparency and to see real faith working in today's world. They want to see a Church with a message that translates into real meaning in their lives. The Church was commissioned to teach a message of real meaning, giving us a destiny and hope. The Gospel is the ultimate relevant message young people are looking for—along with people they can trust to be honest with them as they live out their faith.

Both young adults and youth need to know that they are valued and needed in the local church. They are looking for spiritual fathers and mothers who are real and authentic. As I minister week after week in churches of many denominations, I find that church leaders who are authentic and churches that have learned to incorporate the youth and young adults as a vital part of the local church have lots of youth and young adults in the church. They know they are valued. They are serving on worship teams and in various ministries, and they are vibrant in their faith. And in many ways, they are leading the way. Paul told young Timothy, *"Don't let anyone think less of you because you are young. Be an example to all believers in what you say, in the way you live, in your love, your faith, and your purity"* (1 Tim. 4:12). Who are the young Timothys in your church who are setting the example and leading the way?

Acts 2:17 says:

"In the last days," God says, "I will pour out My Spirit upon all people. Your sons and daughters will prophesy. Your young men will see visions, and your old men will dream dreams."

Young adults and youth will have a vital role in the end-time revival that is coming to our nation.

ENDNOTES

1. Ken Ham and Britt Beemer, *Already Gone: Why your kids will quit church and what you can do to stop it* (Green Forest, AR: Master Books, 2009), 23.

2. "LifeWay Research Uncovers Reasons 18- to 22-Year-Olds Drop Out of Church," LifeWay (survey of 1,023 Protestants, conducted April-May 2007), http://

www.lifeway.com/lwc/article_main_page/0%2C1
703%2CA%25253D165949%252526M%25253D2
00906%2C00.html? (accessed November 3, 2009).

3. Ken Ham and Britt Beemer, *Already Gone*, 31.

4. Mike Matthews with Dr. R. Albert Mohler, Jr., "Does
   Church Need Change?" *Answers*, September 27,
   2009, http://www.answersingenesis.org/articles/
   am/v4/n4/church-change (accessed November 3,
   2009).

5. Mike Sares, "Scum of the Church: How the drive
   for excellence is driving young adults from the
   church," Out of Ur, August 21, 2006, http://
   www.outofur.com/archives/2006/08/scum_of_
   the_chu.html (accessed November 5, 2009).

6. LifeWay, ibid. (accessed March 17, 2010).

7. "Look Out, Here Comes the Gen-X Church,"
   Religion Today, http://74.125.113.132/search
   ?q=cache:F6rq4uoC1PcJ:listserv.virtueonline.
   org/pipermail/virtueonline_listserv.virtue
   online.org/2001-January/001891.html+
   The+generation+of+18+to+35-year-olds,+less
   +concerned+about+structure+and+hierarchy&c
   d=5&hl=en&ct=clnk&gl=us (accessed November
   4, 2009).

8. Dan Lacich, "House Churches, Mega Churches,
   and the Westminster Kennel Club," *Provocative
   Christian Living*, January 27, 2009, http://
   provocativechristian.wordpress.com/category/
   house-churchmega-church-dialogue/ (accessed
   November 4, 2009).

Chapter 3

Emergence of a "Gray" Church
BY ROBERT STEARNS

*"We're not sure who we are or what we believe,
but we're relevant!"*

Each generation puts a new face on everything. Christianity is no exception to this rule. Instead of the plumb line message of salvation through faith delivered by the resolute young Billy Graham, the world could come, in a single generation, to associate Christianity with a feel-good message focusing only on the upbeat, undemanding aspects of faith.

With modernity's concepts of repentance and holiness becoming a distant memory, we are seeing the effects of postmodernism on contemporary Christian culture.

Postmodernity, in contrast to modern rationalism, is very open to spirituality. The spiritual realm is viewed on par with all others and can be seen as valid or invalid; as prevalent or as pointless; as serious or as fictitious, depending on one's personal preferences.

Sensing the need for new ways to reach unchurched generations within this paradigm, many believers started to devise a pop-culture-friendly alternative to the faith, one that is unlike even the mega-church movement with which we are so familiar. Such streams seek to contextualize the

Gospel so that it is conversant with the secular culture surrounding it. With its emphasis on the experiential, the communal, and the applicable, emerging churches have attracted many disgruntled (particularly twenty- and thirty-something) evangelicals.

There are many laudatory aspects of this movement: its quest for authenticity and desire to engage individuals in meaningful relationships with God and others are two such aspects. I want to be clear that God is using in considerable ways many of those who both identify themselves as part of the emerging Church and hold to the fundamental doctrines of the faith. I believe this approach can be a wonderful evangelistic strategy. My concern comes in when the approach is used to substitute as a discipleship mechanism—in other words, when attendance rather than discipleship becomes the goal.

Disciples of Relevance?

Springing up today are self-identifying Christian denominations and movements that sacrifice the values of authentic Christianity to the postmodern virtues of sensitivity, functionality, and above all, relevance.

The last time I checked, relevance wasn't a fruit of the Spirit. For those who place such a premium on looking like, acting like, and sounding like the world, it should come as no surprise that they have no influence *on* the world. They often confuse acceptance by the world around them with actual Kingdom results in impacting their world. It is as though there is a deep insecurity at the root, and they are desperate to prove that you can be "Christian and cool." If Christian radio sounds just like the Top 40, if Christian novels read just like heathen ones, and if church services are no different than social clubs, the question becomes: what's the point?

The problem does not lie in addressing the questions and concerns of the lost in a genuine and accessible way. The apostle Paul did this in Athens, when he artfully presented the Gospel using elements of the existing cultural context as reference points. He appealed to these non-believers in their own language—introducing them to the saving truth of Jesus Christ from the inside out.

> *Then Paul stood in the midst of the Areopagus and said, "Men of Athens, I perceive that in all things you are very religious; for as I was passing through and considering the objects of your worship, I even found an altar with this inscription:* **TO THE UNKNOWN GOD.** *Therefore, the One whom you worship without knowing, Him I proclaim to you…"* (Acts 17:22-23 NKJV, emphasis added).

In his appeal, Paul went so far as to quote secular poetry, saying *"for in Him we live and move and have our being, as also some of your own poets have said, 'For we are also His offspring'"* (Acts 17:28 NKJV, emphasis added). Paul showed how the truth of his message intersected with their spiritual longing.

To be able to speak to the world, showing them how Jesus is as much their Savior as He is yours; to empathize with people's deepest longings for transcendence and give them a Jesus they can relate to by simply saying, "This is that! This is whom you're singing about. This is the One you're trying to pray to. *Jesus* is the answer to your every question and so much more"—that is a gift. I would go as far as to say it is the heart of an evangelist. Is this not exactly what Jesus Himself did when He offered His life to a lost and dying world? We know He was able to speak straight to the heart of the prostitute, the adulteress, the sinner without compromising His purity or the integrity of His message.

Indeed, being relevant is not the problem. However, the obsessive, all-consuming desire to want to be accepted by the world because you are relevant *is!* The minute this becomes our modus operandi, we compromise ourselves right out of our purpose, which is to be salt and light in a darkened world.

If we ourselves do not have the life of Christ emanating from us, if in seeking to be seen as relevant to the godlessness around us we are living in the gray zone of "whatever, whenever, however," then we have nothing to offer the world. Frankly, it would mean that we need as much help as they do. Beloved, if the Church truly *is* the Body of Christ—His Presence and agent of change in the earth today—what could be more relevant?

Nevertheless, this politically-correct brand—or perhaps more accurately, *variant* of Christianity is gaining popularity in the Western Hemisphere, and has the potential to pull even more believers away from a genuine expression of faith in the coming years.

PC Christianity

Imagine the essential tenants of Christianity being run through the sieve of postmodern thought whose mantra is "whatever is true for you is true." What would be left?

In this context (in which anything uncomfortable or unpalatable is pushed behind the curtain in the name of putting on a good show), it is very easy to forget the existence of such tenets altogether.

Christianity's basic tenets will, I believe, come increasingly into question by the organized Church within the next decade. At the same time, there will be a growing acceptance of what would biblically be considered sin—namely sexual promiscuity and "alternative" lifestyles, a devaluing of human life through abortion and euthanasia, a retreating from biblical support of Israel, and a growing tendency to see Jesus as only one of many pathways to salvation.

Believers who profess this brand of seeming Christianity already see themselves as fully Christian, but I believe that, as society becomes increasingly hostile to moral absolutes, they will come to see themselves as *more* fully Christian than their Bible-believing counterparts. After straining out what they see as the antiquated and judgmental aspects of biblical Christianity (aspects the postmodern culture deems unacceptable), these believers will be left with nothing more than the warm, fuzzy residue the rest of the world doesn't mind so much. It is all too easy to see how traditional Christianity could be redefined as something completely nontraditional within our lifetime. In some ways, it already has been.

There are already churches springing up that claim the cause of Christ, yet they distort or dissect the Gospel to create an environment of accommodation in which portions of biblical truth are "massaged" or set aside altogether. This allows for error and sin to be glossed over in a misguided act of "acceptance."

Such churches too often become gaggles of self-described outcasts who claim to love God, gays, and just about everybody else, except Christians. Their approach is based on the belief that if Jesus were on the earth today, we would more likely find Him in the local bar (where these folks meet) than in a traditional church setting.

Surely, Jesus would minister to the lost wherever they might be found. Yet, He would also say "Go and sin no more" (see John 5:14; 8:11). His love would draw sinners into the light and *out of sin.* He would lead them to wholeness by way of holiness, not by carving a pathway around it.

A growing legion of pastors who self-identify as followers of Christ do not embrace a Christian lifestyle. They consider such a lifestyle as being associated with rules and religion, which they consider taboo. Instead, they focus on the "grace" of God, a kind of grace that is taught outside the context of the *full* Gospel.

Some congregations in this vein are quite small; yet they represent a growing subset that is angry at the Church and has decided to leave it and take Jesus with them—or perhaps more accurately, take the aspects of Jesus *that they like* with them. Described below are some of the important truths "churches" like these tend to leave behind.

The Blood of Jesus

Tragically, many who now claim to have a relationship with God no longer see Jesus' blood as the only way to access the Father. It is as though they were seeking to advance the notion of Christianity without its central component. They focus on what they are doing because of Christ (a point with which no one can argue) instead of pointing to what Christ did for them (a topic with which everyone argues).

All the familiar concepts are there, especially the idea of reconciling oneself to God and with others, but we must bear this in mind: without regeneration, there is no reconciliation.

Sin

Those who are more intent on pleasing man than on pleasing God might manage to keep Jesus as the central figure of their spirituality. However, they will filter out any of His teaching that interferes with man's carnal desires. Instead of stepping on someone's toes by pointing out sin, they will focus on the universal principles Jesus espouses, such as equality and social justice. Considering the way a lot of churches talk (or don't talk) about sin nowadays, you might think sin didn't exist.

Instead of having sin in our lives, we have "issues." Instead of repenting, we process our issues. Instead of confessing, we focus on where the issue is coming from. While God can certainly use these processes to get to the root of our sins, we must not forget that our duty is to call sin what it is and then forsake it.

The Authority of Scripture

In today's uber-liberal circles, being a Christian (or at least a certain kind of Christian) can be just as fashionable as being a Buddhist or a New Age pagan. With an emphasis on the subjective rather than the objective, belief in God becomes a matter of personal experience. Whatever feels good, right, or meaningful to you is good, right, and meaningful, period.

Most of us know or have read about self-professed Christians who dabble in belief systems that clearly defy biblical truth. As they entertain their subjective viewpoints, they eventually create "private label" brands of Christianity designed to accommodate their curiosities about astrology, reincarnation, and even astral projection.

In order to do this, the Bible's clear warnings against such dalliances must be willfully set aside. Whole portions of Scripture must be shelved altogether or viewed with sufficient skepticism as to obscure the fact that, regardless of our opinions and interests, sin is sin—and sin has consequences (see Rom. 6:23).

Without giving the entirety of Scripture its rightful place as the compass of our lives, there is no way to navigate through the appealing diversions that beckon to our souls with false promises of comfort, purpose, and fulfillment.

Evangelism

With a shift in focus from message to mission, there is a lot more for adherents to *do* than to *say*. Churches that fall off the deep end of the seeker-sensitive circuit won't share the way of salvation for fear of offending those who don't like the idea of "one way to the Father." It is rather difficult to share the good news of Jesus Christ when you are afraid to assert that God's way is better than Buddha's or Muhammad's or MTV's.

Perhaps the seeker-sensitive in the Body of Christ have kept silent about the truth for so long that they've ceased to believe it themselves. If so, they have nothing left to share but the outward motions of Christian service. While it is wonderful (and biblical) to care for the poor, if these efforts of doing good are carried out as substitutes for *being* good or *proclaiming* what is good, then we have ceased to be the Church and instead have become a kind of Rotary Club.

The Existence of Hell—and Heaven

While it is understandable that some (in their lack of knowledge of God) would feel the need to do away with hell, the new culturally-sanitized version of Christianity also places much less emphasis on the glory of Heaven. When religion is all about the journey, it should come as no surprise that the ultimate destination is no longer deemed as important as it once was. However, Scripture (including the teaching of Jesus) talks extensively about the hereafter—about the terrifying finality of hell, and the electrifyingly-radiant beauty of eternal life in Heaven. It also refers to Heaven as our true home (see Phil. 3:20). A sincere desire to go there should serve as the hallmark of the genuine believer.

Make no mistake about it: the definition of Christianity which has been crystal clear for hundreds of years since the Reformation, is not only under attack; it may have already been redefined to such a degree in America (and elsewhere) as to be beyond our ability to recapture. While there are pockets in the South and Midwest United States where this is not the case, the urban and media centers of this nation have already shifted in what would seem to be unalterable ways.

The good news is that this has happened before. Countless times, especially in the biblical history of Israel, we have seen how one generation, under the leadership of an unrighteous king, can cause a nation to slip into idolatry and become like her pagan neighbors. In the case of ancient Israel, she forgot who she was, and whose she was. Seemingly overnight, she came into great compromise and sin. But God always reserved a remnant and raised up a deliverer.

Again today, in our nation and other nations, we hear the stirrings of a quiet yet resolute remnant that is contending to reclaim our identity as blood-washed sinners who are bringing the Kingdom of God to earth.

Chapter 4

A Cry for Authentic Christianity
by Larry Kreider

*A longing to see the Christian life
lived from the inside out*

In many places we travel across the globe we see a fresh hunger for authentic Christianity. People yearn to see the Christian life lived from the inside out.

Did you ever rush into a department store; gaze down the aisle in search of a clerk; see a friendly, smiling face standing there; and realize it was just a cardboard cutout of a person? From a distance the cutout looked authentic, but it was only an advertisement aimed at piquing your interest. It was not what you thought it was.

We know *authentic* when we see it because it conforms to what it claims to be. In today's Church, there is a cry for authentic Christianity that is marked by integrity and moral uprightness among believers in Christ (especially leaders). The living of consistent Christian lives is essential to that authenticity.

We all know that there are those who "go to church" and resemble Christians, but who lack authenticity. If something is inauthentic, it claims to be one thing, yet proves to be another. I have sometimes said (tongue in cheek) that "going to church does not turn you into a Christian any more than going to McDonald's turns you into a Big Mac."

Without a living, vital relationship with Jesus Christ, people will say one thing and live another. They are inconsistent. Their actions do not match their words. They simply are not genuine. These kinds of characters are rather easy to spot. It is clear that they are not living an authentic Christlike life.

On the other hand, I am sure we all know someone who is a dedicated Christian, someone we respect and look up to, someone we think is above reproach, a person of integrity—who has fallen into grievous sin. Not so long ago, the sad news broke about a well-known pastor and author who fell into immorality. His sin was exposed on the media for the entire world to see. Visible falls like this, especially of Christian leaders, deal a terrible blow to everyone around them. It is sobering and disquieting. When this happens, churches compromise their witness and lives are devastated.

Soon after the very public outing of this man's sin, I made a point to meet with our staff. I looked them in the eye and assured them, saying, "You need to know that I am not involved in pornography and I am faithful to my wife. By the grace of God I will continue to walk in the fear of the Lord."

We can shake our heads in disbelief, but we must be honest with ourselves and seriously ask ourselves the question: Do I have any hidden agendas or sins that I hide because I've convinced myself that they "don't hurt anyone?" Making excuses is the first slide toward compromise.

Paul declared to the church at Corinth that he had no hidden agendas or anything to hide. He was straightforward in how he lived his life before others. He had nothing to be ashamed of, and it was all because of God's grace:

> *We can say with confidence and a clear conscience that we have lived with a God-given holiness and sincerity in all our dealings. We have depended on God's grace, not on our own human wisdom. That is how we have conducted ourselves before the world, and especially toward you* (2 Corinthians 1:12).

No one is perfect. We are all imperfect children of God on a journey of transformation. That is why it is so important to purpose in our hearts daily to walk in purity and integrity. It is a daily task. God has called us to live a holy life. Christianity is not just meant to be talked about; we must live it.

A few years ago, after witnessing the downfall of so many Christian leaders, my friend and colleague Steve Prokopchak and I put together the following list. It gives 25 reasons why we have made the decision to walk in purity and integrity. Make them your own!

- I do not want to sin against the Holy God whom I serve.

- I do not want to deal with condemnation.

- I want to maintain my testimony and my walk with the Lord.

- I want to honor my spouse and my marriage.

- I want to maintain my family and not embarrass them.

- I do not want to disappoint my children and my grandchildren.

∽ I do not want to violate my relationship with other leaders in my church.

∽ I do not want to have to walk away from my ministry position.

∽ I do not want to have to relocate.

∽ I do not want to have to face newspaper articles and the media.

∽ I do not want to hurt my spouse and forfeit our relationship.

∽ I do not want to suffer from overwhelming thoughts and feelings of failure.

∽ I want to be able to sleep at night.

∽ I want to continue to wake up and look forward to a new day.

∽ I do not want to have to face negative consequences.

∽ I want to keep a clear conscience.

∽ I do not want to have to face the law and possible lawsuits.

∽ I do not want to suffer the loss of vision from God.

∽ I want to continue to be able to look others in the eye.

∽ I want to be able to look at myself in the mirror each morning.

∽ I do not want to disappoint those who have looked to me for spiritual leadership.

- I do not want to be the cause of doubt and disillusionment among God's people.

- I do not want to dishonor my church.

- I do not want to cause new believers to stumble or backslide because of my sin.

- I do not want to give the devil a victory.

God doesn't just want us to go through the motions, He wants us to live our lives consecrated to Him so that we can go and bear fruit. He chose and appointed us for that very purpose:

> *The Holy Spirit produces this kind of fruit in our lives: love, joy, peace, patience, kindness, goodness, faithfulness, gentleness, and self-control...* (Galatians 5:22-23).

I believe the Lord is about to pour out His Spirit in an unprecedented way. But to whom much has been given, much will be required (see Luke 12:48). In order for His Church to handle the outpouring of the Holy Spirit that is coming, He requires that our lives emanate the precious fruit of the Holy Spirit. Because His Spirit is holy, we must live lives above reproach, bearing spiritual fruit.

Gifts are given, but fruit is developed. It takes time for a fruit tree to come to maturity and yield a harvest. Fruit grows slowly from within: first the buds, then the flowers, and eventually the fruit. Spiritual fruit grows in the same way as we live each day consecrated to the Lord.

Spiritual fruit is grown in the greenhouse of practical day-by-day relationships with others. The Lord uses the greenhouse of relationships to develop authenticity, patience, and the other spiritual fruit within us. Spiritual fruit is the evidence that Christ truly lives within us. And as we develop love and self-control (the first and last in the list of the fruit of the Spirit), the other seven fruit begin to manifest.

I have often heard it said that many people have enough gifts to get them somewhere, but not enough character to keep them there. Our gifts aren't worth anything if we don't have fruit. And, we never know the quality of the fruit we have until it is squeezed! What do those around you experience when they see you being squeezed by the trials of life? I am convinced that people have an expectation of believers in Jesus: they expect to find good fruit in our lives. The bottom line is that their expectations are legitimate. We *should* expect apples from apple trees.

Are we experiencing the fruit of the Spirit in our lives? If we are truly consecrated to the Lord, we will see signs of spiritual fruit growing. Otherwise, we need to repent and receive grace from the Lord to be truly consecrated to Him, and then begin to grow and bear fruit. The Gospel of John says that we cannot bear fruit just by trying really hard to obey spiritual laws. Instead, we can expect to bear spiritual fruit as we remain connected to the vine (Jesus):

> *Yes, I am the vine; you are the branches. Those who remain in Me, and I in them, will produce much fruit. For apart from Me you can do nothing. When you produce much fruit, you are My true disciples. This brings great glory to My Father* (John 15:5,8).

The Lord is a good gardener! Our responsibility is to stay in a position for the gardener to grow His fruit through us.

Our God desperately wants to invade and revolutionize our personal lives, our churches, our communities, and our nations. Authentic Christianity means a return of obedience to God; therefore the broader harvest is, in many ways, contingent upon our personal obedience to Him. Let's consider the following clear characteristics of authentic Christianity.

A Strong Personal Devotional Life

Authentic Christianity is characterized by a strong personal devotional life for each believer. Nothing can take the place of experiencing time alone with our loving, heavenly Father. Jesus tells us, *"this is the way to have eternal life—to know You, the only true God, and Jesus Christ, the one You sent to earth"* (John 17:3). We get to know Him through personal prayer and time in His Word. A strong personal devotional life characterized the Moravian missionary movement during the 1700s.

> In 1727, the Moravians decided to set aside certain times for continued earnest prayer. Twenty four men and twenty four women covenanted together to continue praying in intervals of one hour each, day and night, each hour allocated by lots to different people. Others joined the intercessors and the number involved increased to seventy seven. They all carefully observed the hour which had been appointed for them. The intercessors had a weekly meeting where prayer needs were given to them. The children, also touched powerfully by God, began a similar plan among themselves... The children's prayers and supplications had a powerful effect on the whole community. That astonishing prayer meeting beginning in 1727 went on for one hundred years. It was unique. Known as the Hourly Intercession, it involved relays of

men and women in prayer without ceasing made to God.[1]

The Lord is restoring this kind of dedicated prayer and hunger for the Word of God in many believers today.

A Desire to Worship Him Only

We worship whatever becomes our primary focus. We can easily fall into the trap of worshiping our jobs, our families, our churches, and yes, even our charismatic expressions of church life. God is calling us to focus on and worship Him and Him only. Imagine inviting your friends and family to your birthday party only to find that no one even notices you are there. We must give God the worship only He deserves in our home groups and weekly worship services. The greatest personal worship of all is to lay our lives on His altar day by day as living sacrifices holy and acceptable to Him (see Rom. 12:1).

A Deep Repentance for Sin

Authentic Christianity always includes a thorough repentance of sin. Our disobedience is not just a problem; it is a sin against a Holy God! David cried out to the Lord after his sin with Bathsheba: *"Against You, and You alone, have I sinned..."* (Ps. 51:4). When we see how our sin grieves a Holy God, we can begin to experience true repentance, which produces pure love. Jesus said to the repentant prostitute who washed His feet with her tears, *"I tell you, her sins—and they are many—have been forgiven, so she has shown Me much love. But a person who is forgiven little shows only little love"* (Luke 7:47).

A Burden for Souls and Evangelism

Authentic Christianity delivers us from being self-centered and causes our hearts to focus on the unsaved. Coworkers and those we meet at the grocery store become souls destined for an eternal hell or an eternal Heaven. When we see non-believers as pre-Christians, we will begin to pray for them and for an opportunity to share our testimonies about Christ, knowing it may be their only opportunity to hear of salvation.

Dependence on Empowerment From the Holy Spirit

Without Him, we can do nothing (see John 15:5). We desperately need the Holy Spirit's power in our lives. Paul told the Corinthians:

> *I came to you in weakness—timid and trembling. And my message and my preaching were very plain. Rather than using clever and persuasive speeches, I relied only on the power of the Holy Spirit. I did this so you would trust not in human wisdom but in the power of God* (1 Corinthians 2:3-5).

When God comes in power, we will never be the same.

Commitment to Fellow Believers and Church Unity

One of the landmarks of authentic Christianity is a holy desire to see the Church as one, just as the Lord prayed in John 17. There is no competition in the Kingdom of God. Pray for other churches in your community. No one church has it all. We need one another. Together we are the Church of Jesus Christ in our region. They will know we are Christians by our love!

Helping the Poor: A Priority

When Peter and Paul affirmed their respective calls to the Jews and to the Gentiles, they made it clear that helping the poor is a priority on the Lord's agenda (see Gal. 2:7-10). Authentic Christianity includes reaching out to the poor—locally, nationally, and internationally. When we help the poor, we are lending to the Lord (see Prov. 19:17). He pays great interest on our investment!

The Call to Missions and the Unreached

The fruit of an authentic Christian life includes an intense desire to reach those who have no Gospel witness. When our hearts are truly touched by the Lord, we find practical ways to help get the Gospel to the unreached. My friends serving in the Muslim world speak of countries that have only a handful of believers in Jesus Christ. God has called us as His Church, to respond to the unreached, both Jew and Gentile, through prayer, giving, and—for some of us—through going.

Lives of Holiness and Integrity

In an age when sexual promiscuity, divorce, and remarriage are rampant in the Church, the Lord is calling His people to walk in a biblical standard of holiness. Marriage covenants must be kept. As believers in Christ, our word must be true. We are called by God to model a standard of holiness, purity, and integrity that makes the world around us jealous.

Perhaps you have been disillusioned or disheartened by the news of an admired leader who was exposed as inauthentic and compromising. Let me give you some good news. For every leader who falls into immorality or any other vice, there are hundreds more whom I meet week after week who love their wives and are not in bondage to pornography, sexual addiction, or financial fraud. There are multitudes of servant leaders in the Body of Christ who love their God; walk in the fear of the Lord; and live humble, accountable lives before others. These are authentic Kingdom leaders.

ENDNOTE

1. "Power from on High – the Moravians and Count Zinzendorf," http://www.openheaven.com/library/history/zinzendorf.htm (accessed April 12, 2010).

Chapter 5

A Hunger to Get Back to Basics
by Larry Kreider

❦❦❦❦❦❦❦❦❦❦❦❦❦❦❦

*Simple priorities every Christian must have—loving
the Lord and loving His people*

There is a renewed hunger in the Church to get back to the basics of Christianity with the simple priorities of prayer, evangelism, and discipleship. Remember what it was like to be a new Christian? You prayed simple prayers of faith and loved reading the Word. You knew you could do nothing without Him. When you prayed to receive Christ and be filled with His Spirit, you took Him at His Word. The Lord honored your simple faith.

He is placing a hunger in the hearts of His people to get back to the priority of loving Jesus, loving His Word, and loving others. Sometimes we make Christianity so complicated; it needn't be that way.

The secret to a fresh, vibrant Christian life is found in staying plugged in moment-by-moment to our power source, Jesus Christ. He is everything we need. If, through disappointment and disillusionment, we begin to leave the simplicity of Christ and trust in other things for fulfillment, we move away from the priorities every Christian must have—that of loving the Lord and loving His people.

Build a Solid Foundation

In the city of Pisa, workers laid the first stone for a magnificent bell tower. The building materials and workmanship were some of the best in the late Middle Ages. Yet it soon became clear that something was terribly wrong: a slight "lean" was visible.

The building's brilliant design was already becoming less important than its flawed foundation. Unfortunately, the tower was built on marshy soil only three meters above sea level. Today, the celebrated "Leaning Tower of Pisa" is well-known as an oddity of architecture.

In nearly 40 years of ministry as a youth worker, missionary, pastor, and servant leader, I have watched this same scenario play out in the lives of God's people around the world. Many start out strong. They launch out in their newfound faith in Jesus Christ with great zeal; yet, they start to sink when they are hit with discouragement and problems. In some cases, I see Christians who have known the Lord for years begin to erect faulty towers, using the building blocks of their personal abilities, gifts, and vision. Unfortunately, their foundations are as unstable as the marshy soil underneath the Tower of Pisa!

Without exception, every one of us desperately needs a solid, biblical foundation for our lives. If a simple walk with Jesus is what we really want, that strong spiritual foundation boils down to three areas of focus: prayer, evangelism, and the making of disciples.

Prayer: Knowing God

God has called us to trust Him, first and foremost! Matthew 28 tells us that Jesus appointed a certain place to meet with His disciples. When they saw Him, they worshiped Him (see Matt. 28:16-18). Jesus has called us to meet with Him and worship Him each day. The Lord tells us in John 17:3 that eternal life is to know Him. Our number one priority must be to trust Him personally, through time spent with Him.

Dr. David (Paul) Yonggi Cho is the pastor of one of the world's largest churches, located in Seoul, Korea. He has spoken to thousands of pastors and church leaders in America in past years. I have heard him say that American pastors are attentive when he speaks on biblical principles that will help their churches grow, but they lose interest and stop taking notes when he begins to teach on prayer and communion with the Holy Spirit.

Often when I speak at churches and conferences, I am unable to take my wife LaVerne with me. I find great joy in searching through my luggage for a special love note that she has hidden in my bags. I love reading those notes, because I'm in love with her. If I no longer desired to read those notes, it would be a warning sign that my love for her is waning. Do you look forward to reading your love letters from Jesus? That is what the Bible is all about. It is filled with love letters from the God who loves us.

Jesus says in Matthew 4:4: *"People do not live by bread alone, but by every word that comes from the mouth of God."* I need a fresh word from the Lord every day. If I am living on last week's manna, I will become weak and even sick, spiritually speaking. Only healthy Christians have something to give to others. We must cultivate our relationship with our Lord Jesus every day.

If your prayer life needs a boost, I would like to encourage you to read my book entitled *Building Your Personal House of Prayer,* and experience an extreme makeover for your prayer life![1] The God-given principles in the book have radically changed my personal prayer life.

Evangelism: Reaching Those Who Do Not Know Jesus

Jesus spent much of His time with the tax collectors and sinners of His day. His heart went out to those who did not live the way God wanted them to.

Ironically, the people who were suspicious of Jesus were not the sinners, but the Scribes and the Pharisees—the religious leaders. If we are not careful, we can begin to focus more on church politics, personal opinions, and self-preservation than on the priorities of Jesus.

The Bible says that *"...the Son of God came to destroy the works of the devil"* (1 John 3:8). The works of the devil are everywhere. Our communities are filled with broken lives, fear, abuse, broken relationships, perversion, the murdering of unborn children, materialism, and lust. Jesus came for the purpose of destroying these works!

Jesus is the answer to every problem. He is the great Redeemer. He came to completely restore every man, woman, and child who will open up their hearts and lives to Him. That is why hearing the Gospel is so important. The Scriptures stress this importance, saying: *"How can they believe in Him if they have never heard about Him? And how can they hear about Him unless someone tells them?"* (Rom. 10:14). We are commissioned by our Lord Jesus Christ to reach those who have not yet placed their trust in Him.

Jesus told His disciples in Matthew 28:19 to *"go and make disciples..."* knowing that all authority had been given to Him in Heaven and on earth. He promised to be with them always, just as He will always be with us. Yet, too often, Christians do not sense the Lord's presence with them. Could it be they are so caught up in the cares of this world that they feel unable to obey the commandment to go and take the good news of Jesus to those who have not yet believed in Him?

Discipleship: Training New Believers

Jesus had a vision of how to revolutionize the world—person by person. Out of the multitudes of His followers, He appointed only 12 to be His key disciples. By living closely with these 12, day in and day out, He gave them intense training, demonstrated His miraculous power, explained His parables, and answered their questions.

A disciple is a learner, an apprentice. Jesus provided His disciples with innumerable opportunities to practice and exercise the things He taught them. For three years, He poured His life into them by close, daily contact.

We must do the same. Whatever He has taught us, we are to teach to others. This not only applies to Bible knowledge, but also to practical Christianity. For example, the most effective way for you to teach a young husband how to love and honor his wife is for you to love and honor your wife. The best way for you to teach another Christian how to have a clear financial budget is for you to show him how you set up your budget. If you believe the Lord has called you to teach a new Christian to pray, then pray with him! We teach others by modeling biblical truths with our own lives.

The Bible offers many examples of discipleship. The apostle Paul took young Timothy with him as a disciple (see Acts 16). Later, Timothy was sent out to take the truths that he learned from Paul and impart them to others (see 2 Tim. 2:2). Moses had Joshua as his disciple for 40 years, during which time he prepared Joshua for leadership. Elijah found Elisha and became his mentor.

The Lord is restoring the truth of loving discipleship to His Church today. He has called us to make disciples. I call this "spiritual parenting"—the nurturing by spiritual parents of spiritual children whose Christian lives can be helped to mature and grow. Through spiritual parenting, we see another's potential in Christ, make ourselves available to them, and thereby make a spiritual investment in discipling them.

This is a fulfillment of the Lord's promise to *"turn the hearts of the fathers to their children, and the hearts of the children to their fathers..."* (Mal. 4:6). Spiritual children need to have the kind of spiritual parents in their lives who will provide the example of character they need and tell them that they are valuable gifts from God. Parents need to help build expectation in the hearts of their spiritual children so they believe in themselves. In my book, *The Cry for Spiritual Fathers and Mothers*, I reveal what happens if spiritual parenting does not take place:

> Too often, in today's church, a Christian believer is encouraged to participate in church services, Bible studies, para-church organizations or evangelistic ministry in order to bolster his faith and "grow strong in the Lord." The theory is that the more teaching from God's Word and interaction with believers, the more spiritually mature he will become.

As important as these involvements may be, such a faulty supposition leads to inhaling message after message, book after book, tape after tape, seminar after seminar, in order to fill a void for real relationship.

A believer becomes fat spiritually and fails to interpret what he is learning so he can pass it on to others. He does not know how to meaningfully and sacrificially impart his life to others because he has never been properly fathered. Without a role model, he remains a spiritual infant, needing to be spoon-fed by his pastor or other Christian worker.[2]

Christianity is not just sitting in a pew each Sunday morning and looking at the back of someone's head. Christianity involves trusting in Christ completely, reaching out to those who do not yet know Christ personally, and making disciples. This must be the motivation of our hearts in order to fulfill the Lord's purposes for us as believers in Jesus Christ.

The three strands of prayer, evangelism, and discipleship take us back to the priorities of Jesus and to the basics of the Kingdom of God. There is a fresh hunger among God's people—those who are totally yielded to Him in intimacy and love—to get back to these priorities again.

Endnotes

1. Larry Kreider, *Building Your Personal House of Prayer* (Shippensburg, PA: Destiny Image Publishers, 2008).

2. Larry Kreider, *The Cry for Spiritual Fathers and Mothers* (Ephrata, PA: House to House Publications, 2000), 4.

Chapter 6

Choosing Authentic Discipleship Over Traditional Church Models
BY ROBERT STEARNS

∼∽∼∽∼∽∼∽∼∽∼∽∼∽∼∽∼∽∼∽∼∽

*Discipling the next generation
in the Word, prayer, and character*

If there is one word that captures the paradoxical cry of the emerging generations, it is the word *real*. Reality television, *The Real World*, finding a "real" person at the end of an automated phone maze. If one thing could sum up what youth and young adults today are crying out for, it is something *real*.

Young people are interested in changing the world in a real way. They are intrigued by the myriad opportunities presented to them by the world. These options tell them they can be a part of something exhilarating and momentous. They're eager to believe and they quickly latch onto the promises of genuine community and personal transformation made to them by such varied outlets as rock bands, Websites, urban gangs, and self-help books.

There is no shortage of passion and ambition within these young people. They are desperate for human connection and yearn for sublime meaning upon which to base their lives—and we wonder why they don't come to church! Youth today are smart, perhaps even cynical. They have witnessed the fruitlessness and, sadly, the hypocrisy that has marked much of the Church in the past several decades. They have decided they want something more.

The Christian Post reports: "Out of 100 American teens, only three are likely to say they see members of the clergy as role models, according to a survey on teens and ethical decision making."[1]

With overall Church attendance on a steady decline and an aging population of those who still attend regularly, many wonder what the future holds. Research indicates there could be millions of twenty-somethings alive today who were active church-goers as teenagers but who will no longer be active in a church by their thirtieth birthday.

Where did we go wrong?

Many within the Body have looked at statistics like these and decided to offer an alternative to traditional church models in order to attract people back into the doors of the Church. In terms of church attendance, they have been largely successful. But is that really the answer? Could it be that what the Church needs to offer the post-Christian world is not something new, but something so ancient, so basic, so intrinsic to our faith, that we have lost it in the frenzy of our modern world?

In His heartfelt exhortation to His disciples recorded in the Book of John, Jesus implored the men with whom He lived, labored, and shared His life, to maintain their connection with the Father through relationship with Him. This was so that they might see the fruit they longed for. His simplicity said it all: *No longer do I call you servants...but I have called you friends...* (John 15:15 NKJV).

Beloved, in our sincere efforts to serve the Lord and advance His Kingdom, have we forsaken the very relationship through which all of this is made possible? Have we gained huge buildings, extensive programming, and refined doctrines, only to lose our best friend?

Everything about Jesus' life on earth was authentic and relational. Unfortunately, those are not the words that come to the minds of unchurched persons when they think of Jesus' followers today. Those words chosen to describe believers are generally more along the lines of *fake* and *judgmental.*

Jesus' intentions toward humanity stand in stark contrast to such negative perceptions. He said, *"...I did not come to judge the world but to save the world"* (John 12:47 NKJV). Furthermore, He never asked people to pretend to be something other than the people they really were. On the contrary, He always found a way to meet people where they were and invite them to a higher level.

The Samaritan woman whom Jesus met at the well was living an adulterous lifestyle, yet did not receive condemnation from Him. Instead, He offered revelation. Jesus crossed numerous cultural barriers in order to show her who He was and how He would give true meaning to her life (see John 4:6-29). It was precisely this authentic, relational approach that defined Jesus' earthly ministry.

As I continue to travel internationally as a guest speaker and worship artist, I notice that discipleship seems to be gaining emphasis within the Body of Christ. If this discipleship indicates a true return to the crux of the Great Commission (which is to make *disciples* of every nation, according to Matthew 28:19), then I take this as an encouraging sign.

I would like to offer us a word of counsel, however, on what I see taking place in the Church. Even the most sincere and well-intentioned efforts at discipleship will ring hollow unless they are based on the true, biblical model. Only that model can succeed.

Would You Like Fries With That?

Everything in our society is geared to the here and now. Every whim and desire known to man is validated by the claim (whether real or fabricated) that those desires can be granted sooner than you ever dreamed possible.

Do you want to lose weight? *Take these pills and drop 20 pounds in one month!*

Do you want to meet someone? *No need to develop a solid relationship; just click on their profile if you like what you see!*

Do you want to earn your degree? *Sign up online and graduate by spring!*

We live in a microwave society that promises to do everything possible (and often what is impossible) before the close of the next business day. The resulting breakdown of relationship, communication, and even our internal thought processes affects our spiritual lives as much as it does everything else.

When you have instant rice, instant photos, and instant knowledge, I guess it seems natural to think you can have instant disciples as well. Discipleship, however, is quite different from a Big Mac. Discipleship requires discipline, intentionality, and time. These are not the values topping the charts these days.

As German theologian Dietrich Bonhoeffer once said, "The test of the morality of a society is what it does for its children."[2] We can see what society at large is doing to our children simply by turning on the television: children are being exploited by the marketing machine at an increasingly young age. But what are we (the Church) doing for our children? Are we offering them a worthy alternative to the hollow enticements of this world; or are we lowering our standards, cheapening our message, and trying to compete for their souls with the same tactics used by those who are trying to lure them away?

As a leader in the Body who has been discipled and who has discipled others for close to 20 years, I submit to you three core areas on which I believe we need to focus in our quest to disciple the next generation—the Word, prayer, and character.

Discipling the Next Generation in the Word

Our Judaic heritage teaches us the supreme importance of God's Word. In this culture, the learner sits at the feet of the Rabbi and memorizes the written Word. As the child progresses, public reading of Scripture becomes part of the learning process. Later, the process includes discussion, reasoning, and application.

In our own culture, there is an urgent need for the Word of God to be given its proper place in the life of every young person and every disciple who desires to walk in the ways of God. Memorization and the public reading of Scripture should be prioritized by every pastor and youth pastor so that we will have the solid foundation on which to build lives of truth and moral excellence.

Discipling the Next Generation in Prayer

The further the Church spirals away from the discipline of sustained, corporate intercession, the further it grows from the heart of God. Prayer that is grounded in the Word of God should be the very bedrock of our spiritual lives, as it was for David and the prophets of old.

Other cultures understand the purpose, power, and unifying force of prayer. For example, the value placed on prayer surpasses the value of all else in the world of Islam. There, prayer is not reserved for a certain few. It is, rather, the common denominator of religious life. How unfortunate that we need to look to those who are not following Christ to learn (if it were possible) what our own loving and personal Savior came to earth to teach us.

Friends, if we are to see God move through us, we must move ourselves to the place of prayer. We must cause those we disciple to internalize the importance of devotional and intercessory prayer and live these out as not just a practice, but a lifestyle.

Discipling the Next Generation in Character

It has been said that character is *who you are when no one's looking.* Character is not what we hope to be or what we think ourselves to be. Character is what we are.

In a society in which the instantaneous is lauded, character is naturally marginalized. It is important to assess what it is that we value, because whatever we value is what we will teach our children to value. Do we value talent or the proper stewardship of that talent? Do we value the anointing or the ability to administer the anointing in holiness and faithfulness?

We must ask ourselves whether we are cultivating in our protégés the kind of diligent hearts and minds that will pursue a life of godliness, or whether we are prizing the end result above the process. In our desire to produce anointed, power-filled ministers of the Gospel, are we half-baking our efforts to the end that the exteriors look "done" while the interiors remain raw?

The fruit of righteousness will not be reaped if it is not sown. Apples do not just appear out of thin air. A seed must be planted and nurtured before a harvest is seen. Are we planting that seed of righteousness by challenging young people to persevere to true spiritual maturity? Or are we putting our energy and resources into artificially manufacturing what appears to be a ripe, gorgeous, appealing apple, but is in fact inedible?

The world is hungry. The spiritually-orphaned youth of this generation are starved for something real, something authentic, something that will nourish their souls. Fast-food discipleship is not the answer.

I want to issue a challenge to you today to enter into intentional discipleship with someone in a real way. Jesus didn't offer anything to His disciples but the truth. Even when they began to forsake Him and claimed His teachings were too hard to bear, He did not compromise the integrity of His message. If we are to fulfill our commission to raise up disciples after Christ, we must be willing to do the same.

ENDNOTES

1. Michelle A. Vu, "Poll: Only 3 Percent of Teens See Clergy as Role Models," *The Christian Post*, February 18, 2009, http://www.christianpost.

com/Society/Polls_reports/2009/02/poll-only-3-percent-of-teens-see-clergy-as-role-models-18/index.html (accessed May 29, 2009).

2. "Dietrich Bonhoeffer—Quotation Details," The Quotations Page, http://www.quotationspage.com/quote/39154.html (accessed May 29, 2009).

Chapter 7

Rising Lawlessness, Societal Chaos, and Harassment of the American Church

BY ROBERT STEARNS

～～～～～～～～～～～～～～～～

Moral absolutes vanish when people are labeled "intolerant" for not approving of sin. Have you noticed the world is coming to an end? I'm not speaking eschatologically, either. Even if you "took God out of it" it doesn't seem like we're much longer for this world. Depending on whom you ask, you will get different answers on exactly why this is.

The environmentalists will point to global warming and the exhaustion of ecological resources such as clean air and water. Due to trends in population and birthrates, social scientists fear the breakdown of civil society and an impending return to feudal factions, mercenary forces, and other antiquated social structures reminiscent of the Dark Ages.

Increasingly, economists are considering the possibility that the world is not only in recession, but potentially on the brink of a full-on financial apocalypse. Individual and corporate greed have taken their toll. No longer able to pacify the monster of debt they created, those we once looked to for direction seem to be leading the entire planet into recession, proving how interdependent all sectors of the global equation have become.

Like a precarious tower built from a deck of cards in which the slightest amount of instability in one area threatens the collapse of the whole, we are collectively teetering on the edge of a doomsday fiscal scenario. We need to brace ourselves for the disintegration of the global community as we know it, and for the resulting geopolitical anarchy.

We live in a world in which:

∽ The decades-long Colombian drug war, which has led to massive, ongoing violence throughout the nation, has displaced an estimated one million citizens, with no end in sight to the country's atrocious living conditions.[1] and being emulated in other heavily drug-trafficked regions.

∽ Mexico, our neighbors to the south, essentially shut down their country to battle a viral outbreak that threatened to become a global pandemic.[2]

∽ A Western European nation (Iceland) went bankrupt overnight.[3] Many believe this will force it into the European Union, inching us closer to a one-world currency.

∽ Many districts of London are now "no-go" areas[4] for non-Muslims. Places within one of the world's major culture centers are now off-limits for women who aren't wearing burkhas and for tourists who are advised by police not to visit due to the religiously fueled hostility running rampant in the streets.

These and countless other factors are setting the stage for the end-time drama unfurling across the nations.

Whenever anything goes wrong on a mass scale, people naturally begin to ask themselves how things got that way. Sensing that the people are so desperate for change that they're willing to compromise (or altogether abandon) conscience and reason, savvy leaders step in and offer solutions the majority wants to hear. Such leaders know the general public isn't interested in or able to fully understand the complexities that contribute to such scenarios, and the much less prepared take personal responsibility for any role they may have had in creating them. Instead, the people too often look for an easy out. They're not looking for solutions. They're looking for a scapegoat.

Intolerant Tolerance

There is a counterfeit system arising in the world, expressed by an alliance between the entertainment, governmental, and religious realms. In this system, everyone ranging from extremely liberal church leaders to the Dali Lama seems to be intent on coming together to affirm one thing: they really don't believe in anything. The only ones not welcomed in the club are those who do believe in something (e.g., moral absolutes). Whether those moral absolutes involve radical Islam or radical Christianity doesn't matter; anyone who isn't vanilla enough to blend into their shake is one and the same. We Bible-believing Christians are being painted with the same broad brush as the radical Islamists who are trying to kill us. In the eyes of staunch secularists, we are extremists, just as the radical Islamists are. Therefore, we are deemed to be part of the problem.

Popular talk-show host and avid opponent of all things Christian, Rosie O'Donnell, expressed this sentiment on an episode of ABC's *The View*, aired in October of 2006. O'Donnell, who also has espoused conspiracy theories regarding the U.S. government's role in the 9/11 terrorist attacks, likened our faith to that of terrorists, saying, "Radical Christianity is just as threatening as radical Islam in a country like the United States." Not surprisingly, researchers found that around one out of every four Americans agreed, to some extent, with her comment.[5]

On a sadly ironic note, the 2009 Miss USA pageant, which one would think should uphold the values that have made the United States of America what it is, seemed to denigrate those values instead. In a move that many people agree cost her the crown, Miss California chose to defend traditional marriage, rather than answer a politically-charged pageant question in a politically-correct manner. The title went to a young woman who later gave an innocuous statement on the controversial subject.[6]

In one generation, society has shifted sharply; whereas being asked such a question was once unthinkable, now it is unthinkable to give a traditional response to the question. Such a response ensures one of being lampooned and vilified as a narrow-minded bigot. Not only is it "offensive" to disagree with the majority, but expressing a minority viewpoint today will cost you!

The 2009 Academy Awards might as well have been an ultra-liberal political rally, with popular actor Sean Penn using the ceremony as a soapbox to voice his radical agenda. Penn's impassioned speech (which received a cheering ovation from those who seemed oblivious to concerns about the breakdown of the nuclear family) was given not only to support a nontraditional marriage proposition in California, but to openly shame those who opposed it.[7]

As if that weren't disturbing enough, an anonymous individual used public Websites to identify and locate those who donated to support traditional marriage in the state. *The New York Times* reported, "Some…received death threats and envelopes containing a powdery white substance, and their businesses have been boycotted."[8] Ironically, this intolerance of opposing viewpoints comes from those who preach the doctrine of tolerance!

The new brand of atheism behind this is not limited to left-wing Hollywood liberals. Some respected scientists holding Ph.D.'s are equally bent on discrediting faith. Atheism is now an aggressive, outright assault on all things God.

The world is looking for a scapegoat, and because it regards "intolerance" as the only sin, Christians are first in line. Even now, there is a marked erosion of civil liberties in democratic nations; these incursions against freedom are made under the guise of maintaining civil order.

Dutch Parliamentarian Geert Wilders is facing abject discrimination after releasing a short film that criticized the Koran, linked it to Islamic extremism, and likened the Islamic holy book to Hitler's *Mein Kampf.* Wilders has been vocal about the "Islamisation" of the Netherlands and the dangers it presents to Europe and the free world. An Amsterdam appeals court has ruled that Wilders is to be prosecuted for "inciting hatred and discrimination."[9] *Inciting* hatred and discrimination? Wasn't Wilders *responding to* hatred and discrimination?

Astonishingly, Great Britain denied Wilders entrance when he flew into Heathrow Airport from the Netherlands. "The British government had warned Wilders he was not welcome because he posed a threat to 'community harmony and therefore public security.'"[10] The real issue is that the United Kingdom, once a bastion of democracy, cannot maintain order in its own streets, which are frequently overtaken by violent Islamo-fascist protesters.

We can see before our eyes an entire continent (now widely referred to as *Eurabia*) bowing down to the duplicitous demands of a politico-religious agenda that knows how to bend, among other things, laws protecting freedom of speech to serve its own advantage. When tolerance is your only virtue, it's amazing how quickly your value system will implode.

Post-Christian Europe has been the first to fall, but Canada does not appear to be far behind. Author and syndicated columnist Mark Steyn's best seller *America Alone: The End of the World As We Know It* attracted unwanted attention from the Canadian Islamic Congress (CIC), which accused Steyn of being Islamophobic.

Ironically, in his book, Steyn points out that "Islamophobia" is a very real and legitimate condition plaguing an increasing number of Westerners who are fearful of falling prey to the murderous and malevolent agenda of a radicalized Islam.[11]

Speaking of irony, Dr. Mohamed Elmasry, president of the CIC, the very one to bring the allegations against Steyn and his cohort, has argued in a television interview that any Israeli civilian over the age of 18 is a legitimate target for terrorist attacks.[12]

So let's see if we have this right: Dr. Elmasry exercised his freedom of speech to call for homicide-bombings of innocent civilians, yet he simultaneously accused an author of hate crimes when that author criticized the terrorism that has come to be associated with Muslim extremists? It often seems that we are living in an alternate universe in which evil is increasingly referred to as good, and good is called evil (see Isa. 5:20).

In Europe, where parents who home school their children are considered to be highly suspect or even criminal, a Swedish pastor was given a prison sentence simply for preaching that homosexuality did not line up with the Word of God.[13]

Light in the Darkness

Faith in God was once the bedrock of Western civilization and was accepted across the board. As it became inconvenient to incorporate the truths of God into a shifting worldview, faith came into question. Next, it came under scrutiny. Today, after being rejected by society at large, faith is seen as an anachronism that is, at best, to be tolerated. More and more, faith is the target of intolerance, more likely to be vilified than respected as forces array themselves against God and seek to expunge the testimony of faith from the earth. Those who live to honor the God of Abraham, Isaac, and Jacob are consequently ostracized from society in virtually every public context.

In the midst of all this, I believe God is issuing an invitation to the brave. I believe He is searching for those men and women who will look on the current crisis with resolve and not with despair. I believe He is seeking those who will roll up their sleeves and hit their knees to ensure that the God of Jacob will retain His rightful place as Lord of all the earth. He seeks those who will stare adversity in the face and say, *"I was born for this."*

    ∾ I believe God is looking for Daniels, whose wisdom and God-given insight will bring light and truth to the dark corners of the world's most corrupt ruling systems.

∾ I believe God is looking for Josephs, whose favor with God sets them before rulers and kings. These believers are entrusted with divine strategies to save entire nations from calamity.

∾ I believe God is looking for Peters—simple, uneducated people who have been with God, and whose faith and boldness have the power to undo religious strongholds and bring thousands into the Kingdom in a single day.

∾ I believe God is looking for Ruths, those who will bind themselves in covenant to the Jewish people, whether unto life or unto death.

∾ I believe God is looking for Esthers, who will count the cost and say, "If I perish, I perish, but I will speak on behalf of God's purposes for my nation and not be silent" (see Esther 4:16).

∾ I believe God is looking for martyrs smeared with the tar and pitch of the world's iniquity, who will burn as lights in the darkness of sin, illuminating the irrepressible truth of the Gospel as the one true pathway to salvation.

God is looking for you. The Lord has need of you. Will He hear you say, "Yes"?

ENDNOTES

1. http://drugwarfacts.org/cms/node/208, (accessed April 21, 2010).

2. "Swine Flu Prompts Mexico Shut-down, U.S. Stockpiling of Supplies," PBS Newshour, April 30, 2009, http://www.pbs.org/newshour/updates/health/jan-june09/flu_04-30.html (accessed May 29, 2009).

3. Michael Mandel, "Iceland goes bankrupt," *Business Week*, October 10, 2008, http://www.businessweek.com/the_thread/economicsunbound/archives/2008/10/iceland_goes_ba.html (accessed May 29, 2009).

4. Michael Nazir-Ali, "Extremism flourished as UK lost Christianity," *The Telegraph*, January 6, 2008, http://www.telegraph.co.uk/news/uknews/1574695/Extremism-flourished-as-UK-lost-Christianity.html (accessed May 29, 2009).

5. The Barna Group, "Rosie O'Donnell Stirs Christians' Emotions," November 13, 2006, http://www.barna.org/barna-update/article/13-culture/143-rosie-odonnell-stirs-christians-emotions (accessed May 30, 2009).

6. Mike Celizic, "New Miss USA weighs in on gay marriage flap," *Today*, April 22, 2009, http://www.msnbc.msn.com/id/30346515/ (accessed May 31, 2009).

7. Douglas MacKinnon, "Tom Hanks, Sean Penn and Prop. 8," *The Huffington Post*, February 25, 2009, http://www.huffingtonpost.com/douglas-mackinnon/tom-hanks-sean-penn-prop_b_169905.html (accessed May 30, 2009).

8. Brad Stone, "Prop 8 Donor Web Site Shows Disclosure Law Is 2-Edged Sword," *The New York Times*, February 7, 2009, http://www.

nytimes.com/2009/02/08/business/08stream.
html?_r=2&ref=technology (accessed May 30,
2009).

9. "Islam film Dutch MP to be charged," BBC,
http://news.bbc.co.uk/2/hi/europe/7842344.
stm (accessed May 30, 2009).

10. "Geert Wilders detained in Britain," ynetnews.
com (from The Associated Press), February
12, 2009, http://www.ynetnews.com/articles/
0,7340,L-3670993,00.html (accessed May 30,
2009).

11. Mark Steyn, *America Alone: The End of the World
As We Know It* (Washington: Regnery Publishing,
2006), 85.

12. "The Michael Coren Show", October 19, 2004, http:
//www.montrealmuslimnews.net/fulltranscript.
htm (accessed May 30, 2009).

13. Keith B. Richburg and Alan Cooperman,
"Swede's Sermon on Gays: Bigotry or Free
Speech?" *The Washington Post*, January 29, 2005,
http://www.washingtonpost.com/wp-dyn/
articles/A45538-2005Jan28.html (accessed May
30, 2009).

Chapter 8

Anti-Semitism and Controversy Surrounding Israel

BY ROBERT STEARNS

~~~~~~~~~~~~~~~~~~~~~~~~~~~~~~~~~~~~~~

The Church today is largely ignorant
of God's enduring covenant with Israel.

There is today an alarming, even terrifying increase of anti-Semitism, just decades after the Holocaust orchestrated by Hitler within Christian Europe. The atrocities perpetrated against the Jewish people (acts which should be unthinkable to any decent human being) are now not only conceivable, but are reemerging in virtually all sectors of the civilized world.

In recent years, the Anti-Defamation League has reported that anti-Semitic incidents are reaching serious highs. National Public Radio confirms that anti-Semitism is on the rise in Europe.[1]

Jews have reportedly fled France because this seemingly liberated, broad-minded nation is no longer a safe place for them to live.[2] Reports of Jewish cemeteries being desecrated and Jewish civilians becoming the victims of violent assaults are now commonplace, as Jews who have called France home for generations find themselves the objects of aggression from the increasingly volatile Muslim youth population.

Since Israel's retaliation in December of 2008 to Hamas' ongoing assault from the Gaza strip, the international community has responded with resounding, across-the-board denunciations of Israeli "aggression." Boycotts, vandalism, violent attacks, and even calls for "death to Israel" are being reported globally, with college and university campuses as no exception.

Academic studies in a number of Britain's most prestigious institutions (in Cambridge, Oxford, Birmingham, and Manchester, to name a few) were disrupted by student protests on par with 1960s anti-war demonstrations. Angry students staging sit-ins demanded that their schools cut all ties with companies linked to Israeli military aid. Not surprisingly, there has also been a corresponding "increase in harassment, intimidation and hostility towards Jewish students," relayed a representative of the Union of Jewish Students.[3]

As we can see, racial slurs, violent demonstrations, and malicious attacks are not limited to the Middle East. The liberal, democratic West lends its own particular variety of racialism to the mix. It is expressed on college campuses, city streets, and even in churches that profess to believe the Bible.

At Christmastime, which is meant to be a season of peace and goodwill, the Church of England approved the singing of a carol in a service in central London that fueled the fires of rampant anti-Israel sentiment within the UK.

They sang the following words set to the well-known tune of *The Twelve Days of Christmas*: "Twelve assassinations/Eleven homes demolished/Ten wells obstructed/Nine sniper towers/Eight gunships firing/Seven checkpoints blocking/Six tanks a-rolling/Five settlement rings.

Four falling bombs/Three trench guns/Two trampled doves/
And an uprooted olive tree."[4]

In addition to being counterfactual, such biased and
bigoted spectacles have no place in egalitarian society, much
less in a house of worship.

Mainstream media, which have never been friends to
Israel, seem to be bent on outdoing themselves in overtly
imbalanced coverage of any conflict involving the fledgling
democratic nation. Every claim made against the state of
Israel, no matter how ludicrous, is given credence and even
front-page status, often without any attempt on the part of
the media to validate the allegation. All the while, the media
turn a blind eye to blatantly wrongful acts continually perpetrated against the state. This willful disregard of journal-
istic integrity and basic morality is anti-Semitism in itself,
and also perpetuates anti-Semitic hatred on a mass scale.

As the world around us becomes increasingly anti-
Semitic, we can see much of the Church tragically seeming
to do the same.

For example, 20 years ago, major Christian media ministries spoke out unequivocally and unapologetically on
moral and social issues, in particular taking a strong stance
in support of Israel. Leaders from divergent streams could
agree on at least one thing: that Christians needed to stand
with God's chosen people, Israel.

Today, however, with a few notable exceptions, it seems
many ministries are silent on such controversial issues,
preferring to project a more appealing, innocuous image of
Christianity. Because of this, many of these ministries do
not stand with or support Israel in any definitive, public
way. What's more, the next generation has been raised on

a steady diet of pluralism, which further erodes the moral bedrock that has, for centuries, served as the foundation of our Judeo-Christian ethic.

The postmodern progeny of multiculturalism has obstructed rational thought and blurred the ability to distinguish good from evil (or even to recognize that there *is* a distinction between good and evil). With emerging leaders who have been conditioned to replace evidence with experience, fact with fable, and "what's right" with "what works," we can already see the results of a culture devoid of sound moral judgment.

There is a popular and intoxicating idea permeating modern society: if we all talk together long enough, we're sure to find a way to get along and enjoy peace. This idea has been widely accepted as Gospel truth. It entirely misses the point that evil *does* exist and will happily engage you in conversation even as it draws within striking distance.

Nevertheless, the next generation, both within and without the Church, rejects the notion of objective truth. Therefore, they cannot see through the web of contradictions woven by those who are eager to take advantage of the stupor pluralism has induced. After all, if no one is allowed to be right, how can anyone be deemed wrong?

It is in this context that we find most of the Church today—at best ignorant and at worst hostile toward God's enduring covenant with Israel.

Israel's Battle

Israel is at war. I'm not referring to the constant rocket fire from the Palestinian territories, the encroaching conflict on the Lebanese border, or the nuclear threats from

Iran (which desires to wipe Israel off the face of the map). All of these clashes are simply physical manifestations of an existential and even spiritual battle that Israel faces alone, in increasing measure.

The tiny nation's resolve to maintain a democracy amid a sea of 22 Islamic dictatorships is a massive demonstration of courage. To all peace-loving, right-minded, and conscientious individuals, Israel should be immediately recognizable as our ideological ally. Instead, much of the Western Church fails to realize that Israel's battle in the Middle East is being waged on behalf of all of Western civilization. Israel, with none at her side, is holding the frontlines of the battle declared against the "infidels" by radical Islam.

Like America, Israel is not perfect. She has made mistakes and I'm sure she will make more of them. But in Israel, Arab women can vote. Arab women can drive. There is religious freedom. There is no call for grandiose geographic expansionism. There is an undeniable, genuine desire on the part of Israelis to live in peace with neighboring nations. Their sincere, sacrificial actions back up this desire.

The idea that Israelis are somehow to blame for defending themselves against constant attacks is popular the world over. Israel was accused by the global community of responding too harshly to attacks from its hostile neighbors. But consider these facts and determine whether such an accusation is founded:

> According to UN figures, in 2005, 1,194 Qassam rockets were fired at Israel (an average of 100 a month), in 2006 the rocket fire increased to 1,786 (an average of 149 a month), and in 2007, 1,331 were fired (an average of 111 a month). According

to Israel Security Agency figures, in 2008, 2,048 rockets and more than 1,672 mortar shells were fired from the Gaza Strip into Israel (this figure does not include the period of Operation Cast Lead, which began on 27 December, during which the rocket and mortar fire increased significantly).[5]

As if it weren't bad enough that the branch has developed such a sense of arrogance toward the root which supports it (see Rom. 11:18), much of the Church does not comprehend that, while Hitler came for the Jews, radical Islam is coming for Jews, Christians, moderate Muslims, and everyone else. While the Church vacillates on its support for Israel, holding to a naïve conjecture that there must be two sides to the story, Israel holds at bay the forces of evil which would (by their own admission) destroy our children in a nanosecond.

Were there two sides to Hitler's story? To Idi Amin's? To Stalin's? No. There were demented, depraved people who had to be stopped. Period. And if, in the end, we refuse to stand against such people simply because the army holding them at bay is imperfect, then it is we who will pay the price.

Battle Plan

After reading this chapter, my hope is that you will agree that doing nothing is not a valid option.

Christians today must come to recognize that Israel is not merely a spiritual entity. It is not an idea or a romanticized, fairy-tale land to sing about. Israel must become a living, breathing reality that is prioritized in the life of every believer. I am often asked by my Israeli Jewish friends how it is that those who care so much about Jesus can care so little for the land of His birth. I can give them no good answer. Not only is Jerusalem Scripture's central city throughout all time, but it is the place of our Lord's soon and sure return. Jesus is not returning to Colorado Springs or Rome or anywhere else but the city of Jerusalem.

If the Bible so clearly illustrates the importance of Jerusalem in the salvation story (both its beginning and its end) why would it drop off the radar of significance in between? On the contrary, God is making Israel a cup of contention in the hands of all nations (see Zech. 12:2) so that, in due time, she might become the praise of all the earth (see Isa. 62:7). We're living in the moment of history that has seen a nation born in a day (see Isa. 66:8) and has seen God's prophecies concerning His covenant land being fulfilled before our very eyes. Everyone who has anything to do with the God of Israel needs to make it his or her business to learn and speak the truth regarding Israel.

Believers need to become educated on any and all issues facing Israel as soon as possible. There are highly effective training programs that offer equipping seminars, informative curriculums, and comprehensive tours of the land, such as the *Watchmen on the Wall Training Program* (www.jerusalemswatchmen.com), which is the only Christian educational program of its kind certified by the State of Israel. Similarly, the *Israel Experience College Scholarship Program* (www.theisraelexperience.com) gives tomorrow's Christian leaders an educated heart for Israel through its rigorous three-week study tour of the land.

I pray that every believer would feel compelled to make a prayer pilgrimage to Israel at least once during his or her lifetime. There is no place like it on earth, and you will receive a special revelation of God's heart and His purposes simply by walking where Jesus once walked and where He will walk again.

Also, every congregation needs to send its pastor to Israel so that the shepherds can gain more insight into how to guide their flocks toward understanding and loving Israel. There are other vital reasons to go to Israel, including support of Israel's economy, which has suffered immensely due to the drop in tourism since the first Jihadist intifada.

Lastly, we must come to grips with the fact that if we will not use our voices, we will lose them. Christians should be politically active in standing for biblical values in all areas, especially in regard to Israel. I encourage you to connect with your local branch of Christians United for Israel (CUFI) at www.cufi.org. CUFI is a grassroots initiative uniting pro-Israel believers around the U.S. Attend "A Night to Honor Israel" in your region, and the annual CUFI summit in Washington, D.C., where you can personally lobby your congressional representative to sponsor legislation that supports Israel.

Friends, the days are short and the need is great. Don't neglect your most critical of mandates to work and pray for the peace of Jerusalem (see Ps. 122:6).

Endnotes

1. Sylvia Poggioli, "Europe Marks Holocaust amid Rise in Anti-Semitism," NPR (audio), January 28, 2004, http://www.npr.org/templates/story/story.php?storyId=1622094 (accessed May 29, 2009).

2. Robert Spencer, "Fearful Jews Fleeing France," *Jihad Watch*, July 29, 2004, http://www.jihad

watch.org/dhimmiwatch/archives/002684.php (accessed May 29, 2009).

3. Olivia Field, "Anger as UK student sit-ins protest Gaza war," CNN, http://www.cnn.com/2009/WORLD/europe/01/30/uk.students.gaza/index.html (accessed May 29, 2009).

4. "Report: Israeli envoy to U.K. accuses church service of being anti-Semitic," *Haaretz*, http://www.haaretz.com/hasen/spages/1045447.html (accessed May 29, 2009).

5. "Attacks on Israeli Civilians by Palestinians," B'tselem (The Israeli Information Center for Human Rights in the Occupied Territories), http://www.btselem.org/english/Israeli_Civilians/Qassam_missiles.asp (accessed May 29, 2009).

Chapter 9

Redesigning and Rethinking Church

by Robert Stearns

*A return to faith unleashing the victory
that overcomes the world*

In the middle of the 19th century, Danish theologian Søren Kierkegaard wrote, "Christendom has done away with Christianity without quite being aware of it."[1] He avidly opposed the prevailing philosophy of his day, which attempted to create a synthesis between logic and faith. He contended that faith was absurd; that it could never make rational sense to the finite mind, and that any attempt to make this radical way of life palatable to the mainstream would compromise the true essence of our faith.

Kierkegaard was right. Not surprisingly, he was eschewed by his religious elite contemporaries, and although his writings would go on to influence many and be regarded as ahead of their time, he died alone and in virtual financial ruin, an outcast of the systematized religious tradition of his day.[2]

As I observe the cultural Christianity of our day, I wonder if I would put it any differently than Kierkegaard did. Indeed, it seems that true faith—*faith-working-through-love* faith—is hard to come by. Many sectors of the organized

Church are, quite honestly, apostate; no power, no authority, no effectiveness are seen in them. In fact, they don't claim to have those attributes or profess to even want them. Sadly, Kierkegaard's words seem to be as accurate today as they were two centuries ago.

The truth is that, in the early Church and ever since—*in fact, now more than ever*—God has been looking for the manifestation of His overcoming Church to expand the Kingdom and usher in the coming reign of our Lord. But the only way He's going to do it is through a people of faith.

Christianity 101

Religion is neat and tidy. It is based on what we can see; therefore, it is easy to trust in. Placing our faith in religion (on what we do because of our beliefs) is a very strong temptation for all of us. Who wouldn't want to have the security of believing that our righteousness is within our own control? How black and white would things seem to be if "being right" with God were encapsulated in simple formulas such as:

- ∽ If I attend x number of services per week, I'll be OK.

- ∽ If I don't do what they're doing, I'll be OK.

- ∽ If my good deeds outnumber my bad ones, I'll be OK.

Faith, on the other hand, is messy. It is based on what we can't see (God). It is for those who know they're not OK, and have no intention of ever trying to be. Faith in Jesus as the One who fulfilled the requirements of the Law is the one authentic alternative to religiously-earned righteousness. *"For in the gospel a righteousness from God is revealed, a righteousness that is by faith from first to last, just as it is written: 'The righteous will live by faith'"* (Rom. 1:17 NIV).

Of course, it didn't take long for this antidote to religion to be made into the biggest religion of all time. Instead of continuing in the radical "otherness" of the New Testament Church, we have largely sold out to pat formulas, easy answers, and man-made strategies.

If you trust in yourself long enough, you will have no need of faith. Eventually, you might find that you can do away with God as well. Tragically, what the world is being offered today is a faithless, Godless Christianity that is easy to accept: no creation, no miracles, no shed blood, no "mess." But the question remains: after you take faith and God out of the equation, where is salvation supposed to come from?

Friends, *the absurdity of our beliefs is the essence of our faith!* It is what distinguishes us from the Buddhists, who try to transcend reality through escaping it; from the atheists who try to deny the truth by rationalizing it; from the new-agers who try to appease the cycle of life by becoming one with it.

We are those who believe a virgin gave birth; we are those who symbolically *"eat the flesh and drink the blood"* of our Lord (see John 6:53). We (many of us) speak in a language that neither we nor any other human ear comprehends. We believe that someone we have never seen, who died on a Roman cross thousands of years ago, is alive and is our Savior. We believe mud and dirt, mixed together in His hands, made a blind man see. We believe that *"to live is Christ and to die is gain"* (Phil. 1:21 NKJV).

The passage in the Book of James that speaks of the relationship between faith and works is often quoted with the intent of emphasizing the importance of works and minimizing the role of faith. However, the apostle was actually making a revolutionary distinction on the causal relationship between the two:

> But someone will say, "You have faith, and I have works." Show me your faith without your works, and I will show you my faith by my works (James 2:18 NKJV).

Here, we see religion turned on its head: our works are to serve as the evidence of our faith, not the basis of it. Instead of thinking we will be saved by what we do, we do what we do *because* we are saved. For followers of Christ, works are an expression of our faith; they authenticate our faith. In light of this, it is easy to see the irony of a Christianity that has placed its trust in its own righteousness instead of in Christ's. While we may be quick to judge with other standards, faith is what serves as God's litmus test; without it, you are not even in the door.

Why Faith?

The end-times battle is a battle of faith. Jesus asked, *"... When the Son of Man comes, will He find faith on the earth?"* (Luke 18:8 NASB).

It is apparent that Jesus, upon His return, will be looking for faith. But why? Why faith? Why is the end-times battle a battle of faith?

I believe it is because faith is the one thing God can't "do" for Himself. Since God exists outside of time, it simply wouldn't make sense to say that God *believes* something is going to happen. He already knows it will!

If you think about it, faith is the only thing we can offer God. He doesn't need our armies, He doesn't need our money, He doesn't need our strategies, He doesn't even need us! The One who created the world and created *you* doesn't need you to give Him anything. The one thing God asks of us—the one thing He is looking for—is faith. And to be clear, He doesn't need our faith so that *He* can overcome; He needs our faith so that *we* can overcome.

> *For whatever is born of God overcomes the world. And this is the victory that has overcome the world—our faith* (1 John 5:4 NKJV).

If you think your victory lies in your having it all together and coming out on top, allow me to give you some brotherly advice: you will never have it all together, and you will never, in your own strength, come out on top. In light of this, First John 5:4 comes as good news. It is not achieving a certain outcome that overcomes the world—it is faith that overcomes the world. Faith is the victory. It *is* the victory! It is not the pathway to victory, the means to victory, or the formula for victory. Faith itself is the victory! The victory is not even found in what we do because of our faith. Instead, the faith that prompts us to do the works we do, *that* is the victory; *that* is what overcomes.

In short, faith is what started it all, and faith is what will finish it all.

> *For this reason it is by faith, in order that it may be in accordance with grace, so that the promise will be guaranteed to all the descendants, not only to those who are of the Law, but also to those who are of the faith of Abraham, who is the father of us all...* (Romans 4:16 NASB).

Like Abraham, we are the arbiters of a divine assault on the possible. Return to faith. Join the revolution.

ENDNOTES

1. Søren Kierkegaard, *Training in Christianity* (New York: Random House, Inc., 2004).

2. Hans Schwarz, *Theology in a Global Context: The Last Two Hundred Years* (Grand Rapids/ Cambridge: Wm. B. Eerdmans Publishing Co., 2005), 47.

Chapter 10

African, Latino, African-American, and Asian Leaders Arise

BY ROBERT STEARNS

Redemptive gifts within cultures and ethnicities are being released in greater ways.

As long as I live, I will never forget my first trip to Brazil to minister at the pastors' conference hosted by Pastor Rene Terra Nova. Twenty-five thousand pastors and their families gathered under a large, very hot tent for four intense days of prayer, worship, and Bible teaching.

To these brothers and sisters, miracles are nothing to write home about. They walk in a realm of supernatural authority not often seen in the West. These people were not just "going to church" together; they were living and building life together. They knew one another's families and were intimately involved in building a Kingdom reality in their community.

Pastor Rene then led a Praise March through the city. Twenty thousand Christians led by this dancing, singing, worshiping pastor overtly declared the Lordship of Jesus and the presence of the Church to the city! I had never seen anything like it in my life. The level of unity in which the Brazilian Church walks is directly reflected in the level of witness they are able to share with their city and nation. Experiencing this made me jealous for more of the things of God to be manifested in my own culture.

The complexion of America and the world is changing. This change holds glorious possibilities for the Church of Jesus as the redemptive gifts within cultures and ethnicities are released in greater ways and cultivated into visionary leadership. In order to realize the full potential of this unique moment in history, these changes must be recognized and welcomed. Then we must sensitively navigate through them so that the flames of God-breathed revival can span across the globe. Consider these examples:

∽ One of the most well-known churches in America, and probably the world, is Los Angeles' Church on the Way. Skillfully pastored for many years by "America's pastor," Dr. Jack Hayford, Church on the Way ballooned into one of America's early mega-churches in the 1970s and 1980s. Though always wonderfully reflective of L.A.'s diverse racial mix, the church nevertheless would have been thought of as primarily an Anglo-populated and Anglo-led congregation. However, as the Los Angeles population changed, something amazing began to happen. "La Iglesia en El Camino" began to thrive! What started as a Spanish-speaking service in 1999 (designed to minister to a minority non-English-speaking contingent of the established congregation) has now burgeoned into a fully-formed Spanish-speaking house of worship with well over 10,000 present in worship each week!

∾ A native Nigerian, Jonathan Oloyede, a respected Church leader from one of the largest black congregations in London is also playing his hand at transforming the continent of Europe. Oloyede has recently stepped away from his pastorate to advance the vision of starting a new, multi-ethnic church model. Although this endeavor takes him well out of his comfort zone, this servant of Christ so values cross-cultural unity that he is stepping out into unchartered territory with an important message for the Body.[1]

∾ Latinos constitute the most rapidly-growing subset of evangelicals, and their voice on important theological and societal issues is growing louder by the minute. Leading the way is the Reverend Samuel Rodriguez, who serves as president of the National Hispanic Christian Leadership Conference, representing nearly 18,000 Latino churches. He was named one of America's seven most influential Hispanic leaders, by a major national news publication and was the only religious leader to make the cut.[2] Rodriguez is playing a key role in the political arena by speaking out on family values as well as human rights issues such as immigration. Elected officials on both sides of the aisle are looking for his input while navigating their way through the quickly-changing landscape of American politics.

∾ The African-American community has risen from the shackles of racism and made an immense impact on this nation and around the world. Heralding this cry for spiritual freedom from the midst of the African-American community is Bishop T.D. Jakes. Frequently on the best-sellers list, this man of God stewards a 30,000 member congregation and is constantly pouring himself out to raise up leaders, entrepreneurs, and healthy families that will continue his life-giving legacy. He is respected globally for his contributions to society and stands as an example of the powerful work of reconciliation God can effect through those who will lead with humility.

∾ Kirbyjon Caldwell pastors the nation's largest United Methodist Church, which, over the past 25 years, has grown exponentially from a membership of just two dozen individuals. He walked away from a promising career in finance to serve the Body of Christ and disadvantaged inner-city residents. He desired to see people break free from oppressive poverty cycles, and founded the Power Center, which offers career help and assists in meeting basic life needs in a run-down Houston neighborhood. His belief that the Church must be active beyond its four walls in transforming society inspired George W. Bush's Office of Faith-Based Initiatives.

∾ In China, I have heard that as many as 20,000 people come to faith in Christ every day. Although such statistics would be impossible to document, the sustained and explosive growth of Chinese Christianity over the past century is undeniably one of most extraordinary phenomena of modern-day spirituality.

∾ It is equally important to note that this fantastic growth (from approximately 1 million Christians in pre-Communist China to more than 100 million today)[3] took place under the iron fist of Communism. These are not lukewarm, apathetic, in-it-for-the-kicks kind of believers. These are people who sign on knowing full well the threat of persecution that awaits them. There is a genuine outpouring of God's Spirit in China; it is being stewarded by courageous and unyielding men and women of faith who are committed to advancing the Gospel with their lives, and if need be, through their deaths.

∾ It is nothing short of amazing to see an Asian population (that the apostle Paul was kept from evangelizing) now substantially evangelized and even leading the way in spreading the Gospel to the unreached. The Back to Jerusalem movement, now headed by the exiled Brother Yun (author of *The Heavenly Man*) envisions sending scores of missionaries to bring the Gospel to Hindus, Buddhists, and Muslims living in the areas between China and Jerusalem.[4]

With Church growth exploding in the developing world while imploding in Western nations, many wonder what this means for the Church, which has long been rooted in places such as Great Britain. More and more, we see places that have served as the bedrock of Christendom shaken and crumbling as they adopt policies and practices contrary to the Word of God.

African bishops within the global Anglican Communion voiced dissent after the consecration of an openly homosexual bishop in New Hampshire in 2003. They felt this was in direct contradiction to biblical morality and discussed severing ties with the Episcopal Church USA. Their opposition to incorporating the homosexual agenda into the Anglican Church has resulted in a controversial halt of such ordinations.[5] While this "arrangement" has not made either side completely happy, it is considered by traditional family-values advocates a step in the right direction.

Once regarded as inferior to the rationalistic faith of industrialized nations, African Christianity appears to be reaching a place of ascendancy. The Archbishop of Canterbury is now taking cues from his colleagues in Kenya and Nigeria. This newfound denominational influence is one of the manifestations of the Church's geographical shift from a European religion to a global phenomenon. The number of Christians in Africa was estimated at 10 million in 1900, and grew over the 20th century to an astonishing 360 million! And this staggering conversion rate shows no signs of dropping off.[6]

As we continue to see God move powerfully in Asia, Africa, and Latin America, as well as in minority cultures closer to home, how should those who have "inherited" the faith of their European ancestors respond?

First, I believe we need to receive what God is doing in our brothers and sisters with genuine humility. We must remember that, as the Body of Christ, we need all our members in order to move forward. Therefore, we must embrace this "newer" branch of Christ's Church, understanding they are as much a part of it as we are. We need to have teachable spirits and not allow our Anglo-Saxon persuasion to constrict our understanding of where and how and through whom God wants to move in the future. It is conceivable that, as sectors of the organized Church become more and more apostate, that true, apostolic authority will transfer to "new" leaders in "other" places. If we desire to move with the Spirit, we will need to align ourselves with these new expressions, even when it means sacrificing our cultural comfort zones.

At the same time, it's important for us to be willing to come alongside these believers and offer them the seasoned insight our heritage and experience provides, in a way which is genuine and not condescending. Sound doctrine, sound leadership strategies, and other life lessons can be vital in helping these new wineskins grapple with their emerging leadership.

Finally, I see this new era of leadership transfer presenting us with an unparalleled opportunity to achieve the kind of Psalms 133 unity God longs to see in His Bride. That place of one accord, with brothers dwelling together in unity, is where God commands His blessing.

Jesus cried out for His disciples to be one as He and the Father were one (see John 17:11); I believe that is a prayer that has yet to be answered. We have seen a measure of functional unity, but not to the degree it is going to take if we want to see the Kingdom advance in our day. If we cannot put Jesus' heart cry for unity above our personal preferences over what kind of songs we sing on Sunday mornings, are we really the radical, end-time disciples we claim to be?

ENDNOTES

1. "A church to reflect the Kingdom," *Christian Today*, February 2, 2009, http://www.christiantoday.com/article/a.church.to.reflectthe.kingdom/22427.htm (accessed May 31, 2009).

2. http://www.cbn.com/700club/guests/bios/ RevSamuelRodriguez121009.aspx (accessed April 21, 2010).

3. http://www.timesonline.co.uk/tol/news/ article5960010.ece (accessed April 21, 2010).

4. http://www.backtojerusalem.com/pages/ vision.php (accessed April 21, 2010).

5. http://en.wikipedia.org/wiki/Homosexuality_ and_Anglicanism (accessed April 21, 2010).

6. "Africa," theWordisLife.net, http://www.wycliffe. net/home/Africa/tabid/423/Default.aspx (accessed May 31, 2009).

Chapter 11

Emergence of Diverse Modern-Day Apostles

BY LARRY KREIDER

There is an increased demonstration, understanding, and recognition of apostles in the Body of Christ.

Through Him and for His name's sake, we received grace and apostleship to call people from among all the Gentiles to the obedience that comes from faith (Romans 1:5 NIV).

Over recent decades, Christ has been restoring apostles to His Church. While the nature and function of apostolic anointing has never ceased, many who served in this capacity were not recognized as such. Some were called missionaries, pioneers, bishops, overseers, and church planters. Yet, many of these Christian leaders were fulfilling the call and characteristics of apostles.

In recent years, there has been increased demonstration and understanding of this gift throughout the Body of Christ. There is diversity in the operation of the apostolic gift. And many younger persons are emerging with this call and anointing on their lives.

For many years, the term *apostolic leadership* was almost nonexistent in churches that operated within traditional denominational structures. In fact, the modern-day Church often divided the ministries listed in Ephesians 4:11 into two groups: the three ministries of evangelist, pastor, and teacher, which were considered as being valid in today's Church; and the remaining two—apostles and prophets—who were believed valid only in the first-century Church.

But times are changing and many churches today believe that the gift of apostle did not end centuries ago with the death of the original 12 apostles chosen by Jesus. These churches believe that God is raising up modern-day apostles who love His Church and who serve as fathers and mothers in the Body of Christ.

If we take a close look at the Scriptures, we see clearly that more than 12 disciples of Jesus were known as apostles. Apostleship was not a closed circle of the original 12. For example, in First Corinthians 15, verses 5 and 8, we see that Christ appeared *"to the Twelve"* and *"then to all the apostles."* This implies that there were other apostles besides *"the Twelve."* Furthermore, Paul actually called many of his helpers *apostles* in the New Testament. Barnabas is one such example (see Acts 14:14; 1 Cor. 9:6).

The circle of apostleship could not have been closed if there were false apostles as mentioned in Second Corinthians 11:13: *"These people are false apostles. They are deceitful workers who disguise themselves as apostles of Christ."* You could not pretend to be an apostle if everyone knew who the only authentic apostles were!

The Scriptures are clear that the 12 original disciples hold a unique place of honor in God's sight. Revelation 21:14 says: *"The wall of the city had twelve foundation stones, and on them were written the names of the twelve apostles of the Lamb."* However, other apostles have been added to the Church to help lead it and make decisions.

There are two basic categories of apostles mentioned in Scripture: The 12 original apostles of Christ, who are in a special category of their own; and other apostles named in Scripture, many of whom did not walk with Jesus during His sojourn in the earth. For example, we read of the following:

- Matthias—Acts 1:23-26

- Paul (Saul)—Acts 9:15; 14:14

- Barnabas—Acts 13:2-3; 14:14

- Silas—1 Thess. 1:1; 2:6-7

- Timothy—1 Thess. 1:1; 2:6-7

- James (the Lord's brother)—Gal. 1:19

- Apollos—1 Cor. 4:6,8-9

- Andronicus—Rom. 16:7

- Junia—Rom. 16:7

- Titus—2 Cor. 8:23

- Epaphroditus—Phil. 2:25-26 (here translated "messenger")

Added to the original 12, this list makes for 23 apostles!

When the Apostolic Is Absent

In Acts 20:29-30, Paul warned the Church of what would happen once he departed:

> *I know that false teachers, like vicious wolves, will come in among you after I leave, not sparing the flock. Even some men from your own group will rise up and distort the truth in order to draw a following* (Acts 20:29-30).

This is a picture of what happens when apostolic ministry is no longer present (this prophecy came to pass after the death of the early apostles).

As early as the second and third centuries, the Church drifted into ceremonialism and tradition. False teaching almost drowned out the truth. Eventually the Church entered the period called the Middle Ages, a time in which the institutional Church gained immense social and political power, but often departed significantly from true apostolic practice and teaching.

The Roman Catholic Church taught that the Church was indeed "apostolic," but that Christ's apostolic authority was institutionalized in the succession (or sequence of appointments) of bishops. From the second to the sixteenth centuries, all the leading centers of the Church had bishops. In the Roman Catholic Church, the Pope, the bishop of the Church at Rome, came to be recognized as the highest bishop of all.

But during the past few hundred years, there has been a growing movement of recognition of modern-day apostles in the Church. In his book *Apostles and the Emerging Apostolic Movement*, David Cannistraci defines an apostle as, "a person who is called and sent by Christ and has the spiritual authority, character, gifts and abilities to successfully reach and establish people in Kingdom truth and order, especially by founding and overseeing local churches."[1]

The apostolic function is inextricably tied to the mission of the Church. We cannot do away with this gift without doing damage to the mission capacities of the Church.

What Does an Apostle Do?

An apostle is one who is sent by God with a mandate from the Lord Jesus to build, plant, nurture, correct, and oversee His Church. Apostles are foundation-layers, the "blueprint" people, those who are "sent forth" (see Eph. 4:11; 1 Cor. 12:28-29; 1 Cor. 3:10).

Dr. C. Peter Wagner further defines what an apostle does by saying that God gives certain members of the Body a special ability "to assume and exercise general leadership over a number of churches with an extraordinary authority in spiritual matters that is spontaneously recognized and appreciated by those churches."[2]

According to the verbiage in Matthew 10:2, an apostle is a *sent one*[3] (see also Luke 9:1; 10:1). This is the word coming from the verb "to send out." Apostles will send the Church forward with an apostolic anointing on every believer.

The Great Commission was given to a small group of people chosen by the Lord, whom He called apostles. Apostles are vital to fulfill the Great Commission today. What is the key? The answer is very simple: They are sent, and the apostolic anointing flows through them to "send" every believer. Only with every believer functioning as a minister will we be ready to overcome the impossible odds that stand in the way of being able to say, "Mission accomplished."

The Initiator of the Apostle's Calling

An apostle is not self-appointed. He is chosen by the Lord himself. Dr. C. Peter Wagner agrees with this assessment: "There is no such thing as a true apostle who is self-appointed. God is the one who decides to whom He wishes to give the spiritual gift of apostle."[4]

An apostle's greatest responsibility is to the Lord who called him. (Please note that here, and throughout this chapter, the male pronoun is used for easier reading. However, both men and women are called as apostles.) However, this call must be affirmed by those whom the Lord brings to Him, by other apostles, and by spiritual leaders in the Body of Christ (see Rom. 1:1; Acts 13:1-4).

An apostolic calling does not automatically mean that the apostle has the right to exercise authority. His authority is by invitation. The church leaders who look to him for apostolic oversight invite him into their realm. His apostleship is proven over time, and they trust his authority and leadership. Remember, apostles are foundation layers and releasers. Their goal is to see the local church succeed. True apostles are not controlling leaders; their ministry is one of giving advice that will lead to success. It is a ministry based upon relationship and exercised within a sphere of influence. In this manner the ministry of an apostle is evidenced by his call from the Lord, the commissioning of his local church, the leaders of his family of churches, and the affirmation of other leaders within the Body of Christ. True apostles are, furthermore, committed to helping to strengthen the local church leadership.

I've heard John Eckhardt say at a conference: "You don't have to force yourself on anyone or try to prove to anyone that you have a gift. If you are an apostle, then as you preach and teach, your gift will be evident. Others in the Body will perceive the grace given to you."

Types of Modern-Day Apostles

There has been much written recently on apostles, but most of what is written focuses on only one or two different types of apostles. I believe there are at least ten different types of modern-day apostles modeled in the New Testament. They have different functions as they exercise the apostolic authority the Lord has given them. Following is a list of ten different types of apostles.

1. The Paul-Type Apostle

The Paul-type apostle is a modern-day apostle sent by the Lord with a vision burning in his heart to establish a family or families of churches. This vision will burn in his heart until he fulfills it. His call is affirmed by other apostles and spiritual leaders in the Body of Christ (see Gal.1:18-22).

He is sometimes referred to as an overseeing apostle. The Lord brings others alongside this apostle to fill in what is lacking in his gifts so the vision can be fulfilled. Paul was called by God to build local churches among the Gentiles, but a team of apostles served with him (see 1 Tim. 1:1-4; Titus 1).

In 1996, the Lord called a group of us to start a family of churches, now established on six continents, called DOVE Christian Fellowship International. I was asked to serve as the international director. Other spiritual leaders in the Body of Christ confirmed to me and to those on our team that my role is to serve as a modern-day Paul-type apostolic leader. We are a new family of churches.

There are thousands of Paul-type apostolic leaders serving in the Body of Christ throughout the nations whom the Lord has used to establish new families of churches.

2. The Peter-Type Apostle

While Paul was called to the Gentiles, Peter was clearly called to minister to the Jews—those who grew up in institutional religion. The Peter-type apostle seems to be a modern-day apostle who is called to minister within the structure of institutional churches. I have many friends who have a clear apostolic call to stay within their long-established denominations and bring change within their conventional structures. Although this has not been my personal call, I admire them for obeying the Lord and embracing a Peter-type apostolic call. Peter and Paul each clearly understood their respective fields of ministry and affirmed one another (see Gal. 2:7-9).

3. The Timothy-Type Apostle

The Timothy-type apostle is a modern-day apostle who is affirmed and commissioned to help fulfill the vision received by the Paul- or Peter-type apostle. A Timothy-type apostle receives his authority from the Lord and from the Paul- or Peter-type apostle who leads the team with whom he serves. He is sent out by the overseeing apostle with specific instructions and mandates that will contribute to the main goal the Lord has given to the apostolic team. His sphere of ministry is given to him by the Lord and by the overseeing apostle with whom he serves. Both Timothy and Titus were sent by Paul to establish elders and oversee churches. Timothy-type apostles become pastors to pastors.

4. The Titus-Type Apostle

The Titus-type apostle is a modern-day apostle who is sent out by a Paul-type apostle to oversee a region. For example, Titus was sent by Paul to oversee the new churches on the island of Crete (see Titus 1:5).

Titus had apostolic authority to straighten out anything that needed to be corrected and to oversee this region. In some denominations this gift is called a "district superintendent or a bishop," but in reality, this person is fulfilling the role of a modern-day Titus-type apostle.

5. The James-Type Apostle

The James-type apostle is a modern-day apostle who has God-given spiritual authority in a city or a local area. Sometimes this type of apostle serves as a mega-church pastor. James was appointed by God to serve the church in Jerusalem (see Acts 15).

He is comparable to many of today's mega-church pastors. He had apostolic authority in the city of Jerusalem. Whenever apostles or church leaders came to Jerusalem, they met with James and the elders (see Acts 12:17; 21:18). I am convinced that most, if not all mega-church pastors, have an apostolic gift from the Lord. This is why it is ludicrous for a pastor to attend a leaders' conference at a mega-church and believe that if he just does everything the mega-church pastor does, he can also lead a mega-church. In most cases, he needs a James-type apostolic gift to lead a large church.

6. The Apollos-Type Apostle

The Apollos-type apostle is a modern-day apostle with a strong teaching gift. Apollos is called an apostle in the Scriptures and he served as an apostle who had a dynamic teaching ministry (see Acts 18:24-28; 1 Cor. 4: 6,9).

Apollos had been given apostolic authority for the ministry of teaching the Scriptures. There are many Apollos-type apostles in the Body of Christ today; they are just not recognized as such. Derek Prince was one; he was an apostolic leader with a global teaching ministry. Derek Prince taught the Scriptures with great authority.

7. The Luke-Type Apostle

The Luke-type apostle is a modern-day apostle who serves in the marketplace. Luke, a doctor, served on Paul's apostolic team sent out to Antioch to plant churches worldwide. He is a model of a modern-day marketplace apostolic minister who serves in business, government, education, the arts, and media. These important apostolic gifts need to be recognized by church leaders and commissioned and released to serve in Kingdom building in the marketplace. We will discuss this more in Chapter 14.

Recently, I ministered at a seminar hosted by Chinese believers in Southern California. They told about a third kind of church springing up throughout China. In the past, there were government-sanctioned churches in China, often called the *three-self churches* (having the three principles of self-governance, self-support, and self-propagation). There were also the *underground house churches* with more than 100 million believers involved in them.

The third type of church in China is the church that is springing up in factories and manufacturing plants throughout the nation. Owners of businesses are starting new churches in their manufacturing plants for the benefit of their workers and the workers' families. Each weekend, hundreds of believers gather together in the manufacturing plant to worship the Lord and receive Bible teaching. These new churches are starting because of modern-day Luke-type apostles.

8. The Barnabas-Type Apostle

The Barnabas-type apostle is a modern-day apostle who is a networking apostle and a true spiritual father or mother. Barnabas was an apostle in the early Church who had grace from the Lord as a networker. For example, when many in the early Church were afraid of Saul due to his background of persecuting believers in Christ, Barnabas saw potential in him. When Barnabas noticed a great need for an apostolic teacher in Antioch, he invited Saul to serve with the Antioch church. And it was here that Barnabas and Saul were sent out as apostles to start new churches in other regions. When the time was right (see Acts 13:13), Barnabas was willing to allow Saul to lead the apostolic team. He was a true spiritual father.

9. The Silas-Type Apostle

The Silas-type apostle serves in a supportive way as an assistant to a lead apostle. Both Timothy-type apostles and Silas-type apostles serve on apostolic teams with a lead apostle, but Silas seemed to be a key assistant to Paul. When Barnabas decided not to join Paul on his second missionary journey, Silas was chosen to go along with Paul as his assistant and companion (see Acts 15:40). Both Silas and Timothy served with Paul on his apostolic team and are often mentioned in Scripture together (see Acts 17:14-15; 18:5; 2 Cor. 1:19). Yet, Silas is always mentioned first. In First Peter 5:12, Paul refers to Silas as a faithful brother who has helped him.

10. The John-Type Apostle

The John-type apostle is a modern-day apostle who can be characterized as an apostle of love. The greatest emphasis in the life of the apostle John was love. This type of apostolic father has great influence in the Body of Christ, but may not fit into one of the other apostolic roles spelled out in this list. However, they are committed to unity in the Body of Christ and they have an ability to cross denominational lines due to their God-given apostolic authority.

One example of a John-type apostle is David du Plessis, who has now gone on to be with the Lord. I remember well, as a young pastor, listening to this modern-day apostle speak with great love for believers of all denominations. He united Catholics and Protestants under the Lordship of Christ. In 1974, a group of Catholic and Protestant editors issued a list of eleven "shapers and shakers" of the Christian faith. David du Plessis was included alongside Billy Graham and other more well-known men and women of God.[5]

Although I have named ten specific types of apostles, not everyone falls neatly into these ten categories. Some apostolic leaders have a gift mix. For example, a mega-church pastor could have a James-type apostolic gift and also be an apostolic-teacher (Apollos-type apostle). He might also lead a movement of churches and have a Paul-type apostolic gift.

Women As Apostles

I believe Junia is a clear scriptural example of a woman in apostolic leadership. The Bible says, *"Greet Andronicus and Junia, my countrymen and my fellow prisoners, who are of note among the apostles, who also were in Christ before me"* (Rom. 16:7 NKJV). Junia was a woman of God. I personally meet dynamic, humble women of God throughout the nations today who are truly modern-day apostles. They have started hundreds of new churches through the grace the Lord has given to them.

This subject of women apostles and women senior pastors is often controversial, but it must be addressed. The debate on the role of women in leadership positions in the Church has caused some churches to split. Inevitably the debate comes down to this question: what, if any, positions of authority can women hold in the Church?

I have found that most church leaders today believe there is no question, biblically and historically speaking, that women can and should be involved in ministering in the Body of Christ. They affirm the need for women's perspectives in ministry and church life in general, and they encourage women to use their gifts. The controversy usually comes in making a distinction between women being involved in using their ministry gifts and women having governmental positions in the church.

At DOVE Christian Fellowship International (DCFI), the family of churches in which I serve, we have licensed and ordained both men and women in ministry. We believe ministry and leadership in the New Testament was a cooperative venture, whose success depended on the gifting and empowerment of both women and men committed to serving Christ and His Church. That's why we see the Bible describing Junia, a woman, in a governmental leadership position of apostle.

However, some of the churches in our family of churches choose to make a clear distinction between ministry gifts and church governmental positions for women. In light of this, we encourage them to discern the Lord's will on this matter for their own congregations. If an eldership team of one of our partner churches believes a woman is called by the Lord to serve in a governmental leadership position and they can affirm her with faith and a clear conscience according to their understanding of the Scriptures, then she will be appointed to serve.

However, Scriptures teach us that whatever is not from faith is sin (see Rom. 14:23). Therefore, if an eldership team of another DCFI partner church does not have faith for a woman to serve on a team due to their personal convictions and understanding of the Scriptures, then they should affirm leaders according to their faith.

As a network of churches we are called to focus on the Great Commission. We prefer not to become sidetracked by differing understandings on a woman's role in church government. Such arguments would divide us and cause us to lose focus. We prefer to honor one another, even though we may not have the same views regarding a woman's role in church government.

Regardless of their individual positions regarding women in governmental church roles, we encourage all of our churches to value the input of both men and women. God created male and female; both are needed and valuable to the Lord and to His people. Male governmental leaders need the female side of the Lord's wisdom that often comes through their wives and other godly women in the Church. Men in leadership should seek out the counsel and discernment of godly women in the Church.

I have experienced too many times in elders' meetings when men have come to a decision, gone home, and then come back to the next elders' meeting to say, "I was praying about the decision we made and I feel we should reconsider." I don't doubt that they prayed; I just know that also they went home and talked to their wives, who had insight from the Lord that they had missed! We need both the male and the female side of God's wisdom to make wise decisions.

The Marks of Apostleship

The proof of apostleship is found in the tangible results: you see the Lord's vision being built and fulfilled and you witness lives being changed. An apostle's field of ministry is limited to that which he was sent to do. He is a spiritual father to the churches he plants. The marks of an apostle are supernatural signs, wonders, miracles, and perseverance. Apostles have the ability to overcome obstacles that would stop most Christians. Luke 18:1-8 and Second Corinthians 12:12 speak about the type of perseverance apostles must have.

Most apostles have been used by the Lord at some point in their lives and ministries to operate in the ministry of the prophet, evangelist, pastor, and teacher. Paul, the apostle, is an example of this truth. An apostle has the God-given ability to walk with the prophet, evangelist, pastor, and teacher, drawing them together in a common vision and purpose.

The Qualifications of an Apostle

An apostle must have the character qualifications of an elder (see 1 Tim. 3:2-7). Christ, the Apostle, came with a servant's heart; therefore, a modern-day apostle must have the heart of a servant (see Matt. 20:26-28).

As a representative of Christ and one sent by Christ to do His work, the apostle must have a father's heart. This means he has a desire to see his spiritual sons and daughters far exceed him in ministry. He will have a heart to release others, and since his work is to build, he is not afraid to release others to the work of God. He sees others as helping to bring completion, not competition, to the ministry the Lord is building. An apostle is willing to sacrificially suffer for the Church. As the father, he gives no thought to himself but is concerned with the vision of God going forward.

Discerning Genuine Apostolic Leadership

Although there are many true apostolic leaders on the earth today, there are also counterfeit apostolic leaders and immature apostolic leaders. Paul spent much time teaching about false apostles in his letters to the church at Corinth. Paul called these counterfeit apostles *"super apostles"* (2 Cor. 11:5) and *"false apostles"* (2 Cor. 11:13). If we can get a clear biblical picture of the genuine, then we can more easily spot the counterfeit. Sometimes the wheat and the tares will grow up together for a while until we can distinguish the difference.

Seven Traits of Genuine Apostolic Leadership

- Genuine apostolic leadership will always build on the foundation of Jesus Christ. They point us to Jesus, not their pet doctrines or methodologies (see 1 Cor. 3:10).

- Genuine apostolic leaders love the Body of Christ and grieve over division in the Lord's family (see 1 Cor. 1:10; John 17:21).

- Genuine apostolic leaders are spiritual fathers and mothers who desire to serve and release the next generation (see 1 Cor. 4:14-17).

- Genuine apostolic leaders walk in the supernatural (see 2 Cor. 12:12).

- ∾ Genuine apostolic leaders are patient and do not quit (see 2 Cor. 12:12).

- ∾ Genuine apostolic leadership's authority is expressed through servanthood (see 1 Thess. 2:6-8).

- ∾ Genuine apostolic leaders know their boundaries as set by the Lord and honor the spiritual fields of others (see 2 Cor. 10:13-17).

True Apostles, the Next Generation, and Spiritual Families

Many modern-day apostles will establish spiritual families within spiritual families. In his book *Fivefold Ministry Made Practical*, Ron Myer says:

> God is raising up many modern day apostles who love His Church and who serve as fathers and mothers in the Body of Christ. These apostles have a desire to train and raise up church leaders to come to maturity, to release them, and then move on to plant another church. Their greatest joy is to reproduce themselves in their spiritual children as they parent them to adulthood. Apostles are spiritual entrepreneurs who love change and relish finding new ways of doing things. They are always coming up with new concepts and new patterns. They are willing to take chances, and at the same time willing to change. They are not satisfied with "the way things are" but burn with a greater vision for the church.[6]

The apostolic anointing keeps the Church from being outmoded and outdated. It keeps us relevant to our world, without compromise. Without apostles, some denominations (under bureaucratic or administrative leadership) have crystallized and failed to adapt to changing culture, society, or opportunities to advance the Kingdom of God. Modern-day apostles are the catalysts in advancing the Church and taking it to new ground.

ENDNOTES

1. David Cannistraci, *Apostles and the Emerging Apostolic Movement* (Ventura, CA: Gospel Light, 1996), 91.

2. C.P. Wagner, *Your Spiritual Gifts Can Help Your Church Grow* (Ventura, CA: Regal Books, 1979), 208.

3. Biblesoft's New Exhaustive Strong's Numbers and Concordance with Expanded Greek-Hebrew Dictionary. CD-ROM. Biblesoft, Inc. and International Bible Translators, Inc. s.v. "apostolos," (NT 652) and "apostello," (NT 649).

4. Matthew D. Green, ed., "The Doc Responds" (chapter by C. Peter Wagner), *Understanding the Fivefold Ministry* (Florida: Charisma House, 2005), 31.

5. The Website of Holy Trinity New Rochelle, NY, "David du Plessis," Jonas Clark, *Spirit of Life Ministries*, http://www.holytrinitynewrochelle.org/yourti19217.html (accessed April 12, 2010).

6. Ron Myer, *Fivefold Ministry Made Practical* (Lititz, PA: House to House Publications, 2006), 57

Chapter 12

The Widely-Emerging Regional Church

BY LARRY KREIDER

❧❧❧❧❧❧❧❧❧❧❧❧❧❧❧❧❧❧❧

*The walls are coming down! The Body of Christ
is beginning to work together.*

All over our nation, God's leaders are finding one another! From the East Coast to the West Coast and
in hundreds of places in between, pastors and Christian leaders are realizing that the Kingdom of God is much
bigger than their own churches or ministries. They are beginning to experience the fulfillment of the prayer of Jesus
that we may all become one as He and the Father are one
(see John 17:11). In the following pages, I will share just a
few examples of how God is sovereignly bringing His people
together in practical ways in towns and cities in our nation.

Regional Church: Lancaster County, Pennsylvania

Forty years ago, the walls were high between churches
and denominations in my county—Lancaster County, Pennsylvania. Rather than experiencing the unity Jesus prayed
for in John 17, there was competition and skepticism among
churches and pastors. There was a great need for believers
in Christ to see beyond themselves and their local churches

to come together and work for the good of our region as we learned to love one another and love our neighbors as ourselves.

Believers who had God's heart for unity prayed. They kept on asking and seeking and knocking. Believers from churches and ministries in Lancaster County forged new paths by praying together. Over a 40-year period, we prayed in small prayer groups in homes and in church buildings alike, seeking authentic biblical unity. We had a seed of hope in our hearts that we could strategically serve one another to bring about the revival of life and faith that we knew was needed in our region.

Today, by the grace of God, the scene has drastically changed. Many like-minded believers in our county of more than 700 churches (including a multitude of persuasions and denominations) see themselves as The Regional Church of Lancaster County (www.theregionalchurch.com). The walls are coming down. Pastors of diverse denominations have become true friends. We are the result of decades of intentional prayer and of relationship building. It's a testament to the power of esteeming one another in love (see 1 Thess. 5:13). It is a story of long-term unity and solidarity that gives a Christ-centered witness to others.

Steps Toward Transformation

In the early 1980s, I was a young pastor with very few relationships with pastors outside my own denomination. I had grown up in the Church of the Brethren, married a Mennonite pastor's daughter, and led a team who started an interdenominational church for new believers who were coming to Christ. But I felt isolated from most of the Body of Christ in our county. I simply did not know many of the local pastors on a personal basis.

However, I knew of a man named Sam Smucker, another young pastor in our county who was leading The Worship Center, a new rapidly growing congregation. His Amish background intrigued me. The two of us decided to meet for lunch. I was amazed at how many things we had in common. We each had a strong desire to see pastors and leaders pray together for revival and transformation in our county.

We discussed the possibility of starting a monthly prayer breakfast for pastors and other Christian leaders. We were told by other pastors that this had been tried in the past and no one showed up. In spite of this, we took a step of faith and started an interdenominational monthly prayer breakfast at a local restaurant. It went on for years without any fanfare. Every month, an assortment of interested church leaders met to pray on behalf of our region.

This group (typically 15 to 25 pastors) spent time in fellowship around breakfast and prayed for unity, revival, and a general spiritual awakening to visit our county. We kept it simple. Sometimes we had 75 pastors coming to pray and sometimes there were only five or six of us. At times, we considered quitting, but God gave us grace to go on.

As pastors, we had no agenda other than anticipation for revival and unity. We sincerely believed that the many local churches in our county had something to offer one another, and we envisioned submitting our gifts and strengths together for a higher, collective good. We desired to work and pray together for the ultimate spiritual and social transformation of Lancaster County. Our deepest desire was to encourage and help equip the whole Church so that it could grow and mature in Christ.

It was inspiring and enlightening to realize that despite our differences, we could cooperate, accept, and affirm one another in a powerful expression of unity.

Breaking Down Barriers

As we prayed consistently over the years, we became increasingly convinced that our doctrinal distinctives should not keep us from experiencing unity and enjoying our commonality in Christ. In prayer, we chose to release our self-centered attitudes that stood in judgment of the theology and practices of our fellow Christians. Instead, we opted to focus on relationship building and getting to know those outside our own churches or denominational circles.

Doing that is never easy. When leaders from diverse settings start meeting together, they have to make a concerted effort to lay down their egos, titles, roles, statuses, and agendas.

When Sam and I started this gathering, we made a decision to keep the prayer meeting pure from personal agendas. There would be fellowship around breakfast and prayer for revival in our region—that was it. There were no announcements about upcoming conferences or visiting evangelists at any of the local churches. We came together around two things only: fellowship and group prayer for revival. Those wanting to share about their special meetings were invited to place brochures on a designated table.

Out of this regular prayer meeting, friendships were built. Pastors and their spouses began to meet together socially with their counterparts as trusting relationships developed.

We believed that God intended for our county to display the maturity and unity that is possible in the Body of Christ. Our heart's cry was to see churches of many different denominations strategically serve together to revitalize the Church and give a Christ-centered witness to the communities around us. We envisioned the blessing that comes when God's people corporately turn to Him and acknowledge Him in all their ways.

Increasingly, the leaders in our region recognized the immense value of gathering together as a group. Our coming together helped to meet our needs for relational accountability and friendship. As we connected with one another, we shared the load of leadership. Trust grew. Ethnic barriers began to fall. The separation between churches in the city of Lancaster and the county as a whole began to decrease. We found a safe place to discuss problems and encourage each other, as well as learn from each other's mistakes. We were there for one another.

Today, small groups of pastors, intercessors, and leaders from many denominations continue to meet for prayer throughout our county. A house of prayer, including laborers in prayer from more than 30 churches, is praying around the clock. A county-wide prayer strategy is being formulated, an evangelism team is coming together, and the vision necessary to sustain relational networks for each of the seven spheres of influence within our county is in place. From these solid relationships, The Regional Church of Lancaster County is emerging.

Keith Yoder, a leader with the Regional Church of Lancaster County, made this comment to me:

The oneness for which Christ prayed develops progressively. What began as praying together led to relational trust. Trust became the foundation for unity to be expressed in corporate gatherings of the Church in communities and county-wide. Unity opened the way for partnerships to emerge for ongoing cooperation in ministries of compassion and benevolence. We are now poised to partner strategically to communicate the Gospel of Jesus Christ to every resident in our county.

We still have a long way to go, but God has begun a good work in our county. We are convinced He is committed to fulfilling that work.

Regional Church: Kelso-Longview, Washington

More than 20 years ago, International Renewal Ministries' founder, Joe Aldrich, led a Pastors' Prayer Summit. He called together over 30 leaders from the Kelso-Longview area in Washington state.

This endeavor to promote unity among regional churches had a bumpy start. Mark Schmutz, a Baptist pastor and one of those leaders, recalls how the meeting was marked by great divisions among the pastors of the community:

> Pastors would actually rebuke one another in their prayers. Dr. Aldrich is noted to have declared in utter frustration, "If I had a bus, I'd put you all on it and send you home!" Thankfully, they remained together and began working on developing authentic biblical unity.

> It hasn't always been easy, but the Prayer Summit will convene again in 2010 for the 22nd year.

The Prayer Summit model birthed a weekly local Prayer Group that has been meeting ever since its inception in 1989. Many of the pastoral leaders of our community have testified that it is the love and unity birthed in regular prayer together, with and for one another, that has, at times, been a major factor that has helped them remain in ministry when they felt like abandoning the call.

In recent years, the prayer group has undergone a transition into a Leadership Prayer Group as it has expanded to include leaders at any level within the church and community ministries of the region. The Prayer Summit, held in the spring of each year, has also expanded to include fall and winter retreats as the level of unity has deepened and become something leaders long for on an even more regular basis at more intimate levels. It is open to leaders at every level in the church and regional ministries.

The fruit of these times together has led to the mobilization of the church of the community to meet needs through an annual week of service called *Servant Week*, responding to the expressed needs of our city governments. The strength of relationships has also helped church leaders respond quickly in a unified way to advances into the community by various groups misrepresenting the Gospel. Out of the bond created in prayer, these leaders are able to work together to quickly rally the Body of Christ in the community to respond to urgent needs and issues.

These leaders have also regularly walked together to pursue the Lord's purposes for their community. Spiritual mapping, organized prayer-walking, and other community-wide prayer initiatives have been birthed out of this group. We established daily prayer watches and launched the Three Rivers House of Prayer (TRiHOP), presently operating 24 hours each week. The unique expression of this house of prayer is that it is not just one congregation facilitating this prayer ministry, rather it is the unity of several congregations participating together in sustained, informed intercession. TRiHOP is also the venue for regular city-wide events, such as hosting leaders in the Body of Christ from around the world and the local ministerial association.

Out of this profound level of unity, the Prayer Summit of 2008 identified three apostolic leaders who now function to provide leadership within this movement in the region. While this fledgling group is still discovering what this call means and how they are to function for the sake of the health of the Body of Christ in our community, it is beginning to show signs of fruitfulness.

While this movement is small—a remnant of the whole Body of Christ in the region—they have learned, by persevering, not to despise the day of small beginnings. [1]

Regional Church: Reading, Pennsylvania

Just like God answered Elijah and Israel by fire, Christians in the city of Reading, Pennsylvania, believe their journey in city transformation has been marked with God's fire. They began with just a few pastors and Christian leaders meeting weekly on a mountain overlooking their city, repenting and praying for a move of God to sweep through their city and county.

Early one morning in those initial days of prayer together, a literal fire alarm rang out. Craig Nanna, a local pastor, and others were praying for God's Spirit to be poured out upon the land and signs to be seen, including *"wonders in the heavens above and signs on the earth below—blood and fire and clouds of smoke. But everyone who calls on the name of the Lord will be saved"* (Acts 2:19,21).

Craig described to me what happened next:

> In a matter of moments, a fire truck roared up the mountain toward us and stopped beside our little outdoor prayer meeting on the mountain. When we inquired about the emergency, fire personnel stated, "A fire has been spotted from below, right where you are standing." We assured them that we were only some pastors praying for God to bless our city.

This experience profoundly stirred the hearts of this group of pastors. They were convinced that if only God's people would pray, He would surely forgive and heal the land.

Now, more than ten years into this journey, they have grown into a relational network known as the Reading Regional Transformation Network (RRTN). They are committed to pursuing and preserving the *"unity of the Spirit"* (Eph. 4:3 NIV) as one Body of Christ in the Reading region, without competition or comparison.

Their pursuit is the unity of the Spirit and not the spirit of unity. The former is focused on a joint dependence and total reliance on the Holy Spirit as central to transformation in their region. The latter brings with it man's attempt at coming together with unity as the central theme. At best, such an effort often results in a watered down, powerless "Christian" ecumenicism.

One of the group's favorite times together occurs when they close their doors on Sunday morning and all come together in one location as the City Church with every tribe and tongue worshiping the One who sits on the throne. They meet in the park, the arts center, or at different church sites. Their corporate gatherings stand as a witness to the community that there is one Body, one faith, one Lord.

They are committed to keeping prayer foundational because prayer clarifies whose kingdom they are building. They do not come together for their own limited agendas or ideas, but simply to pray. As they seek God, His agenda comes forth and His Kingdom is built without end. As numerous churches and believers come together seven days a week from all across the region to build a House of Prayer, they are seeing the signs of an open Heaven over their city and region. Once called one of the most dangerous small cities in Pennsylvania, the crime reports in Reading are now showing a dramatic decrease.[2] Coincidence? They don't think so. They believe it is God's response to the praying church.

As they have continued in relationship and unified prayer together, various strategic initiatives have come forth as catalysts for transformation in their region, including evangelistic outreaches, combined water baptisms in the Schuylkill River, international conferences, and an "Awake Reading" day of prayer for their city called by the county commissioners. Just last summer, the praying church of Reading (over 30 churches and 300 volunteers) in conjunction with

Nicky Cruz Ministries invaded the darkest corners of their neighborhoods every night for two weeks. More than 1,000 people committed their lives to Christ. Dramatic Acts 2 accounts of conversions occurred. One night a young man was sharing the Gospel in English while an onlooker who only knew Spanish miraculously received the translation and gave her life to Christ. God spoke to another man in a dream to visit a church the following Sunday and commit his life to Jesus.

I believe God wants us to realize that He has given us stewardship of regions; therefore, we must work together with others in our regions. We should no longer be content with building our own personal kingdoms and success stories. God has placed His people in a region to develop and bring His Kingdom expression to impact every aspect of that area. No one ministry or church can accomplish this alone. As Christian leaders, pastors, business people, educators, government officials, broadcasters, filmmakers, and publishers, we must come to this realization. As we do, we'll learn to work as one to cause a region to continually reflect more of God's Kingdom.

These are only a few examples of a growing movement of believers and church leaders who are honoring one another and seeing the Kingdom of God as being more important than their own churches and ministries.

Endnotes

1. Mark Schumtz, as told to Larry Kreider, November 11, 2009.

2. "Reading, Pennsylvania," http://webcache.google usercontent.com/search?q=cache:3_-QTg GVlTAJ:en.wikipedia.org/wiki/Reading,_

Pennsylvania+Reading,+pa-+the+most+danger
ous+small+city+in+Pennsylvania%E2%80%9D
&cd=2&hl=en&ct=clnk&gl=us (accessed April
12, 2010).

Chapter 13

A New Release of Intergenerational Ministry

BY LARRY KREIDER

~~~~~~~~~~~~~~~~~~~~~~~~~~~~~~~

*Spiritual fathers and mothers are picking up
the mantle to nurture younger Christians.*

God is turning the hearts of the fathers to their children and the hearts of the children to their fathers (see Mal. 4:6). Intergenerational ministry is a renewed trend in many parts of the Body of Christ. It is beginning to happen, and it is refreshing. The Church is moving from a season of control to a season of release!

Imagine a Christian more mature than yourself giving you a hug and saying, "I see God's potential in you. I want to stand with you for the long haul and see God work in your life." After the initial shock wore off, how would you react? By giving a hug back and shouting "Hallelujah"?

If you are like most Christians, another sermon on Christian living isn't going to scratch your spiritual itch. What you need is more of the Lord, along with a mature, compassionate "father" or "mother" to parent you spiritually.

This is a subject near and dear to my heart. As I travel throughout the world, training leaders week after week, I see a consistent and desperate need for this kind of intergenerational connection—for spiritual fathers and mothers to nurture younger Christians so the old and the young can walk together and learn from each other. I firmly believe God has called believers to mentor intergenerationally; that's why I wrote the book *Authentic Spiritual Mentoring.*[1]

Mentors or *spiritual parents* are those who are willing to help others grow up in their Christian lives. They help to fulfill the Lord's promise to *"...turn the hearts of fathers to their children, and the hearts of children to their fathers..."* (Mal. 4:6). Although this Scripture has implications for our natural families, its significance for spiritual parenting in the Church is profound. Without releasing spiritual fathers and mothers in the Church, we are in danger of losing the next generation.

As a young pastor's wife, my wife LaVerne struggled in the early days of ministry because of the pressure she felt to conform to the expected pastor's wife role of organizing women's groups, meetings, and programs. As she tells it, "I knew I was not going to be the typical pastor's wife who played the piano or the organ or sang. I just did not feel called to occupy my time with being a public person. I knew God did not call me to spend my time heading committees and planning women's events. My heart's cry was to be a servant of the Lord Most High. Every time I got down on my knees, I knew what God had called me to do. It was clear: train a few women at a time."

LaVerne spent the next few years doing just that. She started to pour her life into a few of the women who were small group leaders in the church. It wasn't a job for the fainthearted. The relationships she developed took time and effort. She was not standing up front to an adoring public; she was behind the scenes, giving of herself day by day to others.

For years, she simply trained women in the background, out of the limelight. She loved these women as she inquired how their marriages were faring. She prayed and wept with them as they went through life's hard spots and rejoiced with them when they experienced life's joys. This kind of spiritual mothering had far-reaching effects. These women were equipped to pass on to other women the impartation they had received. There was a multiplication over and over again of LaVerne's initial efforts with a few women.

Today, LaVerne continues to mentor women one on one. When she speaks to larger crowds, the heart's cry of women is often: "But where are the older women? Where is that spiritual mother who will mentor me and help me grow up in my Christian life?"

With tears streaming down their faces, younger women are saying, "Sometimes I could use just an hour of a spiritually mature woman's time. I so desperately need to be encouraged to look to the Father. I need to hear from someone who has spiritual maturity beyond mine—someone who can teach me valuable lessons from life."

What the younger generation is looking for is a friend, a coach, a cheerleader, a mentor who can point them to Jesus.

Understanding Generational Differences

Understanding the values and needs of each generation helps us to understand each other and work together. This working relationship is a challenge for today's mix of generations. It does not happen automatically.

For example, the older generation values hard work, conformity, and respect for authority. The baby-boomer generation grew up questioning authority. The twenty-somethings of today belong to part of two overlapping generations—the "iGen" and "Gen Y" who have many distinctions from young adults in the past. In their lifetimes, the Internet boomed. They are technologically savvy, achievement-oriented, creative, and impressive multi-taskers. And, they are looking for real-life role models and mentors who can show them the way.

When the great mix of generations learns to understand each other, accept each other, and forgive each other, they can build healthy, vital relationships. Every believer, young and old, is important and useful in God's Kingdom. Mentoring relationships provide a powerful avenue of involvement for everyone.

Certainly, multi-generational situations within the family and Church are bound to generate conflicts. Sometimes it is a struggle to speak each other's language, or understand each other's worldview. But tensions can be lessened when each determines to use his or her strengths to help each other's weaknesses. An intergenerational connection often requires using our imaginations to interact in new ways. Each of us must be willing to claim our unique roles, share what we know, and pass it on.

Mentoring "Unplugged"

When it comes to spiritual parenting, many potential spiritual mentors wonder, "How could God ever use me to be a spiritual parent? I have a lot to learn. What if I make mistakes? Am I really ready for this?" Mentoring the next generation takes transparency and a willingness to be real.

You don't have to have all the answers or be a super-spiritual, flamboyant, "amplified" Christian. A simple "acoustic" Christian is fine!

At the Last Supper, Jesus took off His outer garment and knelt down and washed the disciples' feet, saying, *"I have given you an example to follow. Do as I have done to you"* (John 13:15). Before you can serve others, you must take off your "outer garments." Although an outer garment is usually cast off when you are ready to get down to some serious work, you can also look at the outer garment as a metaphor for the Sunday-best behavior you must cast off.

Sometimes this outer garment is a cover-up to hide our vulnerabilities. We don't want others to see our weaknesses, so we keep our outer garments pulled around us, intact and stiff, getting in the way of genuine experiences with others.

It can get complex and risky when we open up our lives to others. But honesty is humbling and liberating. A performance mentality goes out the door when we share our real, uncloaked lives with others. Uncloaked, we no longer mentor because we think it is required of us, but because we love as He loved us.

No matter what you do—whether you are a homemaker, student, factory worker, pastor, or the head of a large corporation—you have the divine blessing and responsibility to mentor others, who will in turn impart to others the rich inheritance God has promised. This is true intergenerational ministry.

Release Them!

Many years ago, Dr. Cho, the pastor of the world's largest church in Seoul, South Korea, spoke at our pastors' conference in Pennsylvania. I was stunned at his evaluation of much of the American church. "American pastors are afraid to release their people," he told me.

Providentially, during the past several years, a divine transformation has begun to happen in the hearts of many pastors in our nation. Pastors are being changed from spiritual CEOs to spiritual fathers and mothers, training and releasing their spiritual sons and daughters.

Only a dysfunctional parent will try to hang on to his children and try to use them to fulfill his own vision. Healthy parents, both naturally and spiritually, are committed to encouraging and empowering their children to help them fulfill their God-given vision. They expect their children to eventually leave their home to start their own families.

Today's generation is a digital one. Information streaks across the globe at lightning speeds through Google. The world is changing fast—some of the change is for the good and some for the bad. Digital technologies are changing our young people in ways we don't yet understand. Moreover, the current generation of young people in our churches has experienced brokenness—broken homes, divorce, and abandonment. This generation also lives in a time of a grave global financial crisis, terrorism, natural disasters, and AIDS.

But our God has amazing dreams and ambitions for today's younger generation. God's people in First Kings 20 experienced a major victory against their enemies when the older leaders released the younger leaders to lead the way into battle. God always makes provision for young people to serve the purpose of God for their generation.

How can we effectively disciple this generation while providing space for them to discover and then walk their own spiritual paths and journeys in Christ? I firmly believe that we must give young people four things that they long for: time, love, authenticity, and truth. Young people want someone who is "for real" to listen to them, to walk with them through the good and the bad, and be there to encourage them, challenge them with truth, and pray with them.

Jesus spent most of His time with His disciples, who were thought to be mostly young men in their early 20s, and some even younger. In fact, He chose John to be His very closest disciple; Bible scholars believe John was the youngest of them all.[2] Peter, James, and John were His inner circle with the remainder of the 12 also being close at hand. Additionally, He took time for the 72 in His larger circle. Jesus' style of disciple-making has been all but lost in many parts of the Body of Christ. Yet it really is the simple way that Jesus reproduced Himself in His followers, starting with the one disciple who was the youngest.

Now here is my question for you as you face your future. Who will your "disciple John" be? Paul and Timothy really grasped this truth of disciple-making when Paul told Timothy:

> *Timothy, my dear son, be strong through the grace that God gives you in Christ Jesus. You have heard me teach things that have been confirmed by many reliable witnesses. Now teach these truths to other trustworthy people who will be able to pass them on to others* (2 Timothy 2:1-2).

Paul exhorted Timothy, who was his disciple, to find another reproducing disciple who would disciple another.

I want to issue you a challenge that has the potential to change the world. Ask God for one reproducing disciple within the next few months. Just one! Sure, if you want to disciple more, go for it as God gives you the grace. But start with one and encourage your "disciple" to disciple someone else next year. Then the pattern will repeat as, every year, you each find another person to disciple who is also a reproducing disciple. In ten years, by just discipling one person each year who also disciples one person, you will have been responsible for the discipling of more than 1,000 people!

After 20 years, at just one disciple per year, how many disciples do you think you will be responsible for? Over one million! That's right, over one million in 20 years, at the rate of just one person each year. Do the math if you do not believe me. After 30 years, the number jumps to over one billion!

No wonder the enemy has been hiding this truth from the Body of Christ and keeping us busy in activity—even religious activity. Now for the naysayers and doubters who are saying, "But we do not live in a perfect world. What if our discipling plan breaks down?" My response is simple, "I will gladly 'settle for' half a million disciples if the plan breaks down."

Jesus said it like this: *"...the good seed represents the people of the Kingdom..."* (Matt. 13:38). And the principles of the Kingdom are found in the parables of the sower (reproducing 30-, 60-, and 100-fold) and in the parable of the mustard seed, a seed so small, yet with such vast potential!

Our God is calling us to a new level of commitment to the dynamic truth of disciple-making. Recently, I published a two-book biblical foundation series entitled *Discovering* the Basic Truths of Christianity and *Building Your Life on the Basic Truths of Christianity.*[3] These books are practical tools to help you disciple the next generation by taking just one chapter per week over the next year and discussing these vital foundational truths with your "John" or your "Timothy." When you help others with the basics of Christianity, guess what? You will also receive renewed faith from His Word to live victoriously above the struggles of daily life.

No matter how talented or experienced you are, if you want to excel at anything, you must practice the fundamentals—the essentials. It's true for playing the piano, it's true for playing baseball or golf, and it's true for the Christian life. Discipling a young person will bring you back to the basics of Christianity again and again.

So, this is my challenge to you as you approach this next season of your life. Find your "John" or your "Timothy." Who is your Second Timothy 2:2 reproducing young disciple going to be?

Let's believe God for a new wave of church planting in our nation and in the nations. We must expect that our spiritual children will be used by God to birth new types of churches that will fit the needs of their generation. Every generation has a need for its own wineskin. Many in our generation are starting new house church networks in communities throughout our nation.[4] Regardless of the structure of the new wineskins, God has called us to be spiritual parents who help our spiritual children fulfill their dreams for their generation.

A sweeping revival is just around the corner. God's people need to be alert in order to accommodate the great harvest this will bring in the Kingdom of God. Spiritual parents will need to be ready to obey His call and take these young Christians under their wings. And new "spiritual families" need to be formed. The Lord wants to bless all of us with an awesome spiritual inheritance.

ENDNOTES

1. Larry Kreider, *Authentic Spiritual Mentoring* (Ventura, CA: Regal Books, 2008).

2. "How old were the disciples of Jesus Christ during their ministry?", http://wiki.answers.com/Q/How_old_were_the_disciples_of_Jesus_Christ_during_their_ministry (accessed April 12, 2020).

3. Larry Kreider, *Discovering the Basic Truths of Christianity* and *Building Your Life on the Basic Truths of Christianity* (Shippensburg, PA: Destiny Image Publishers, 2009).

4. Larry Kreider, *Starting a House Church* (Ventura, CA: Regal Books, 2007), 1.

Chapter 14

The Kingdom of God and Marketplace Ministry
BY LARRY KREIDER

~~~~~~~~~~~~~~~~~~~~~~~~~~~~~~~

God calls, trains, and equips Christians to not only serve in the Church, but also in business, education, media, athletics, entertainment, and civil government.

There is a clear trend today that is focusing in a renewed way on the Kingdom of God. The Gospel of the Kingdom is not the same as the Gospel of the Church. The Gospel of the Kingdom changes lives and transforms communities through the family, the church, business, government, education, the arts, and media. The Church is obviously very important to the Lord, but it is only one aspect of the Kingdom of God.

Jesus said, *"…The Kingdom of God is near! …believe the good news!"* (Mark 1:15). The Kingdom of God is good news! Religion causes people to focus on rules and regulations and their outward performance instead of an inward change. The Kingdom of God transforms individuals, families, towns, cities, and nations from within.

Although the Kingdom of God includes the Church, it is certainly much bigger than the Church. It includes everything under the reign of God. If God is reigning in your business, you have a Kingdom business. If God is reigning over your family, you have a Kingdom family. If God is reigning over your church, you have a Kingdom church.

I recently witnessed God's Kingdom influence in amazing ways during a visit to a new church near Kisumu, Kenya, the birthplace of President Obama's father. At Restoration Church, in the village of Kadawa, I saw firsthand a village of 10,000 being transformed by the Kingdom of God. The church is less than two years old and already has over 500 people coming together each Sunday as hundreds have received Christ. In fact, they have already planted two new churches from this newly established congregation.

But the most amazing thing is the way the entire community is being transformed by the Kingdom of God. Believers are starting new businesses, the swamp in the region has become a banana plantation, and the main government leader of the village and his whole family have been transformed by Christ. He told me that his job is now easy because violence and mugging have stopped in the village. Hope has been restored. This is the first year that they can remember that no one has contracted cholera in their community. There are signs of Kingdom influence everywhere!

George Eldon Ladd (1911-1982) was ahead of his time in his groundbreaking book entitled *Gospel of the Kingdom*. A professor at Fuller Theological Seminary, he defined the Kingdom this way:

> The Kingdom of God is basically the rule of God.... God's reign manifests itself in both the future and in the present and thereby creates both

a future realm and a present realm in which man
may experience the blessings of His reign.[1]

In the introduction for the book, Oswald J. Smith explains
Ladd's understanding further, saying, "The Kingdom...is
a reality...that is destined to dominate the whole world."[2]
Smith goes on to say that "God's government demands complete submission. His subjects must put Him first."[3]

More than 25 years ago, I heard Loren Cunningham,
the founder of Youth With a Mission, speak on "seven mind-molders" of culture—forces that shape society and the nations. In fact, God spoke to Loren and to Bill Bright, founder
of Campus Crusade for Christ, at the same time concerning
these seven areas, and they met the next day to compare
notes. They discovered that there are seven main spheres of
influence that shape a nation or a city, and these "molders of
culture" hold the keys to global harvest.[4] They are:

- Family
- Church
- Business
- Government
- Education
- Arts
- Media

As Christians, we are called to transform our culture.
We are the influence of Christ in the world. People, cultures, and countries are affected by our influence. Jesus and
His disciples affected the culture around them and transformation happened. The 120 Christians in the Upper Room
in Jerusalem 2,000 years ago have grown to 1.2 billion or
more and have impacted the culture of every nation where

they have flourished. We are called to be salt and light in our areas of influence.

In his book *The Seven Mountain Prophecy*, Johnny Enlow discusses how we have been assigned to influence these seven foundations of culture (mountains):

> Today, nations with no history of Christian political leadership are coming under the influence of Christian presidents, congressmen, and other key governmental leaders. Christian educators are being drawn to the forefront and becoming known for new concepts and new curriculum for schools. Movies and art are suddenly experiencing Christian influence as never before. Christian athletes, coaches, artists, musicians, economists, lawmakers, journalists, entrepreneurs, and the like are being spiritually promoted like never before. As the world becomes darker, the true light of Christ is beginning to shine brighter. In unprecedented fashion, the church is getting an opportunity to manifest Christ's solutions for society—in an "outside the four walls" context. The Lord is raising His people up and giving them an opportunity to fulfill the entire Great Commission—to disciple nations and not just individuals.[5]

Enlow believes that for years the Church has spent so much time focusing on the Church that we have forsaken our responsibility to the world. The Kingdom of God is so much larger than what the Church has addressed in the past.

My friend Lance Wallnau says we have looked at the call to go into the world and bring in a harvest of souls as our main point of focus (a quantitative goal). But he says we have a qualitative assignment also, which is to transform nations and make disciples of the nations. Dr. Wallnau teaches on "The Seven Mountain Strategy," which explores seven strategic areas of influence in society that shape the culture of every nation, and how a great world harvest can be reaped if Christians infiltrate and capture these vital "mountains."[6]

In light of how Christians should prepare to take the lead in society, there has been an increased interest in the Kingdom of God and "marketplace ministry" within the Church. Christians can fulfill their desire to serve God in the workplace as God connects their jobs, businesses, ministries, and life purpose into one package. People now understand that only a few believers will ever serve in a pulpit while most Christians will find their God-given calling in diverse ways in the secular world. This is more than the latest Church fad; it is a genuine move of God that is transforming the Church to become a powerful, practical strategy to disciple cities and entire nations.

"There must be a uniting of church leaders and marketplace leaders to fulfill the purposes of God, and we must make every effort to do so," according to Ron McKenzie in his book, *Being Church Where We Live*. He goes on to say:

> A Church with an apostolic vision will train people up and send them out to work in the business world. The Kingdom of God expands as Christians extend the rule of God into areas of life where they have authority. Authority is an essential aspect of any kingdom. This means that Christians should seek positions of authority to help the Kingdom to expand.[7]

My friends, LaMarr and Nancy Esbenshade, started a greenhouse wholesale business in the 1960s. As a Christian couple, they always tried to keep God at the center of their lives and business and share their faith with their employees, customers, and salespeople. But they continued thinking of their business as a secular career. When they finally realized that they were not only to give money to ministries but they were themselves a full-time ministry in the workplace, they gained a new perspective. They realized being in business was not a lower or higher calling than any other office or profession in life. It is making a difference wherever God has placed you.

Eventually, they hired an intercessor to come and pray a couple of days a week at their business. They covered every employee in prayer. They made personal counseling and prayer available to employees, customers, and salespeople. They helped employees when they got into financial problems. This couple found their God-given calling in the secular world in marketplace ministry.

Our God is a King who is building His Kingdom in our lives and in our communities. He has always been about transforming nations and causing groups of people to know Him. He wants to use each of us as His tools to accomplish His purposes.

To which mountains has God called you to exert Kingdom influence? There are seven spheres of influence that shape and change culture and society throughout the world, and whoever influences these seven "mountains" helps shape and control what takes place throughout our towns and cities and nations.

During recent years, believers in Christ have come to realize anew that God has called them into these spheres of ministry. They have been trained and equipped to serve Him in educational institutions, media, print, radio, television, the Internet, art, athletics, entertainment, business, science, technology, and civil government at many levels. When believers know they are called to these specific Kingdom spheres and they pray and serve together, each honoring the call and spiritual fields of others, transformation begins to happen.

We need each other. Let's together seek first the Kingdom of God and His righteousness, and He will add all things to us (see Matt. 6:33).

ENDNOTES

1. George Eldon Ladd, *Gospel of the Kingdom* (Grand Rapids, Michigan: Paternoster Press, 1959, reprinted 2000), 24.

2. Ibid., 11.

3. Ibid., 12.

4. Retake Your City, "What are the 7 Mountains?", http://www.retakeyourcity.com/mountains.html (accessed April 12, 2010).

5. Johnny Enlow, *The Seven Mountain Prophecy* (Lake Mary, Florida: Creation House, 2008), 10.

6. "Interview with Lance Wallnau," *Prophetic TV*, August 2006, http://prophetic.tv/watch.php?e=12 (accessed October 28, 2009).

7. Ron McKenzie, *Being Church Where We Live* (Christchurch, New Zealand: Kingwatch Books, 2004), 156-161.

Chapter 15

A New Movement in Prayer
BY CHUCK D. PIERCE

~~~~~~~~~~~~~~~~~~~~~~~~~~~~~~~~~~~~~

*A prayer movement needs to be the wine
for the wineskin that is forming.*

From state to state in our nation, mobilization has begun again. However, this time the connections are different: apostles are praying, prophets are prophesying with clarity, and intercessors are birthing the future.

Not too long ago, the Lord clearly said to me that *"the prayer movement needs to be the wine for the wineskin that is forming."* He revealed to me that as the apostolic government of the Church matures, the prayer movement has to stay fluid and remain new as a drink offering to their region. He showed me new people in every state who are to be involved. He showed me how many of you had been faithful in the past season, but how you will need to expand your connections.

An apostolic governmental anointing in the prayer movement has now emerged. As we draw closer to the end-times and see spiritual warfare intensify, we need to pray in such a way that we may receive revelation for the battle and live in such a way that we withstand the schemes of the enemy.

The Lord sovereignly positioned me with Mike and Cindy Jacobs at the beginning of the 1990s. I was a prayer warrior, and Cindy was an intercessor. She has had great influence in my life. I listen closely when she prophesies to the prayer movement. Recently she spoke the following:

> It is time to shift the prayer movement. We must become apostolic in our expression. We must find the intercessors and the prophets and align them with the apostles in each state. If each leader of the present movement will shift, their state will shift. If this shift does not occur, the Lord's Kingdom will not be established from state to state and a nation will suffer greatly.[1]

Prophets must mature in their prophesying. Here is a question I have asked many: Are you wine or a wineskin? Do you flow predominately in the category called wine (revelation), or are you developing a wineskin for others to pour into? If you are wine, what are you being poured into? Where are you being poured? If you are a wineskin, who pours into you?

God is raising up a Kingdom army full of prayer warriors who know their spheres of authority. We are being sent again! We must embrace the shifting paradigms that are being communicated this hour from Heaven. We must assist in the development of strategies to unlock the nations of the earth.

God will use this peculiar people in the earth to change the way His Kingdom advances. Are we still praying? The answer is a loud "Yes!" The army of God is growing stronger and stronger daily.

Ask the Lord to renew your prayer life. Pray with words and pray the Word! Travail and pray without words. Pray in the Spirit with words unknown. Commune with your Maker and be bold in the earth realm where you have been positioned as a witness to His love, grace, and power. Speak and decree the Word. War with your prophecies. Do not let the confusion around you create a veil of darkness that stops you from moving forward.

Protect Your Vineyard!

There is a new call to watch the vineyard you have been given. Protect your vineyard from the many enemies[2] that would rob you from seeing His blessing occur during this hour in your life! Political structures could rob you of your inheritance in this hour.

Recently, before I was to lead a prayer gathering, the Spirit spoke to me and said:

> "Protect your vineyard! Get it cleared, plowed up, and ready to plant. I am removing one hedge to build another. Ask Me to remove the seeds that will produce wild grapes, rebellious structures, and iniquitous thrones in your portion that you have been allotted. Be a watchman over your portion. I am watching over the earth and reviewing My plan of fullness. I am changing the horizon line of My people! Their vision must shift to see what I am seeing. There are enemies in the land that I must now address or the land will be overtaken and its productivity for the next three generations lost. I am going deep to pull up roots that will produce rebellion in days ahead. My people will be revolutionary in a time of lawless rebellion! Declare

that the uprooting has begun in your house, your land, and the industry you are part of. Thank Me for the uprooting of seeded, twisted, unfruitful systems and structures that could prevent My Kingdom people from becoming radiant in the future.

"I am passing out new assignments! I am causing you to hear what I am assigning you to. Some will be assigned to nations. Others will be assigned to kingdoms, others to companies, others to churches, and others to cities. I will assign some to one person. He or she will open up your future as you pray for them. New assignments are coming this hour.

"Ask God to get you ready and positioned for new assignments!

"See the fields I am calling you to. Many will be called, placed, and planted in new fields. From these new fields you will see the boundaries I have for your future. Many of these fields are undefined. I will show you where to build a hedge.

"I have begun to tear down hedges! I am reestablishing the fields of harvest for days ahead. While tearing down the hedges, I am uprooting the plants that will not produce the fruit for the future. This is a time to pluck up and pull out. I am setting you in these opened up fields to be My farmer for this season. Learn the laws of harvest. Some of you will be plowers and some will be reapers. Many walls were built high in the last season around fields that I had planted, but wild grapes came up. Now I must tear down old fortresses and cause old structures to fall. I will begin to go in now and redo fields. You have been trying to secure the fields from the past season! But now, hedges are falling and the fields that you have been working hard to secure will be re-plowed and planted with new grain. They will have a new form of harvest. They will be plowed in new ways.

"Get ready, because in your confusion, the tearing down is part of the process. When I asked you to go forth into the fields the last time, I found you under a shade tree saying, 'Why, Lord, are You doing things this way?' I am moving you out from under the shade! Shake off your self-pity and allow My light of revelation to fall on you. Some of you are feeling exposed. You are not sure where your boundaries are because I am changing them. New fruit is being developed. I can re-graft, prune, and graft again to produce new fruit from old vineyards.

"Do not kick against the pricks! The new boundaries and assignments that I am forming around you are key for you to submit to. You had no idea what it would look like when I began to remove and re-seed the earth for the harvest ahead. I am beginning to do that. I am giving out new assignments for prayer. You must get your assignment and pray for new industries to form. You must pray during this reorganization of industry. Do not just hang onto your job but come to Me in these days of changing structures. I must transplant and redo the many industries for many iniquities have been held in the industries that produced the movement of the last season. Now I must redo. Some of you are going through a great emotional crisis in your process of being transplanted. Wait! Do not wither in this season. Your roots will go downward and produce fruit upward.

"There is deeper oil that I am searching to bring forth. It has been held for the season ahead. I must go at a different angle to penetrate into and catch that oil and bring it forth. Don't be afraid to invest in the deeper drilling. It will produce a flow that will sustain you in the next season. Like Jonah who went and sat under the shade tree, some of you have not liked what I am doing. I have used you to prophesy to set an order and to create a tearing down and uprooting. You have gotten upset in the changes around you. I will dry up what you are hiding under. Rejoice in the changes I am bringing that will produce great fruit in days ahead.

"I am calling forth rivers of Healing! Many of you have not been able to see the river. Rivers that have nourished crops and brought healing have dried up. My people must find My healing river! I will shake up the fields! I am shaking up your field! The river is hidden. It is very deep. Deep must call to deep. The river must rise again! There must be a river of healing in certain fields before I can move forward. You have turned toward healing. Your healing process is creating a great shaking. This shaking is tearing the walls of the vineyard. Now new vineyards must be established. The river of My power was captured in the last season. A war formed over the movement of the river, and the river became a dry bed. I must watch for the times to break the captivity of the healing river.

My healing river must flow into new areas to heal the people and the earth.

"New instruments are forming! You did not understand the type of instruments I would need in this season. In My reforming, you have not understood what you are going through. I am making new instruments to plow new ground. You must change your vision at this time for your field and assignments are changing. Also, My instruments are changing. I must plow up ground that had wrong seeds, wild roots, and bad fruit. The land is crying out to produce its harvest but you must allow Me to purify the land. 'If My people who are called by My name will humble themselves and pray and turn from their wicked ways and seek My face, then I will hear from Heaven and forgive their sin and heal their land.' You have entered an uprooting season and roots that have been hidden must be found. Your days of communion are changing. Your prayer life will take a shift. Let Me show you how to pray in different ways, new ways. Your English roots are on the verge of changing. The root structure will affect you. Ask Me to cause a wall to be torn down and removed. You are dealing with little foxes and I want to change the whole field. The little foxes will crush the grapes and I have got to plow the whole field again. There will be a healing move in those of Scottish descent.

"Do not despise small beginnings! There are new seeds I will sow in those fields. They will come up and look small, but will become very fruitful in days ahead. Some of you are not seeing the smallness of the seed that I will plant to cause things to happen. A different vine must be released to produce the fruit for this season. This is a season of pruning and grafting and re-grafting. Do not focus on the plant. If you are looking at the plant, you could align with Saul, who had 'the look.' The top of a plant is not the key since the vegetable that nourishes it is down under the dirt. You must learn to see and eat the root that has gone deep. If you are not careful, you will focus on the Saul system and look from appearance as opposed to the stream and the root of Judah that must spring forth this hour. I must shift you for you are operating out of eyesight as opposed to seeing My root blessing. I am moving from one layer and I am going deeper.

"You have been speaking from the surface of your emotions, but I am going deep into the very depths of your heart so you speak forth. Even the songs and the prophecies and that which I have given you have been at one level, but now I am going down into a place that you have never had unlocked. It will nurture what I want to produce this hour. I am unlocking the next song for you to sing. I am going deeper to unlock a valve and connect with a river that will produce a different type of song.

"The furnace of My fire is much greater than hell's lickings. I am causing you to go into the kiln of My process at this time to fire you and make you glazed and radiant so that I can use you as a vessel in days ahead. I will fire nations this year. I will cause things to happen that will create a furnace in nations. In the midst of that happening, I will bring forth those that are tested and tried. Do not balk when I assign you to be at the ticket counter at a toll booth. Yes, you have great abilities, but there is a reason I have placed you there. Quit despising your position so that I can rebuild the hedge of the place where I will plant you in days ahead.

"Bless Me at every small beginning. You will see that there was a river producing nutrients at one level but there is a fire that is down deep that will cause germination to occur. Where hell has licked your feet and your process from the last season, you will see the fire of hell and will know how to distinguish it in the flow of the fruit that I will bring forth in the next season. I will bring forth songs that will quench hell's fires in the next season. My people are not aware of the changing structures, and are grieving and in denial because the structures are changing. I am going to go deeper to produce the songs to show them the depth that I can bring forth on their behalf.

"The fruit of the blessing is in the root. This is why I prune the fruit and branches. What needs to be lopped off in appearance will be lopped off. You have looked at the appearance, but I am going deeper so that the blessing is connected rightly and will come forth in a new way. The blessing is the fruit that grows from the root. When your root goes deep and draws from the river of My anointing and presence, My blessing cannot help but come.

"I will pluck up certain things this year and leave other things in the ground. I am digging and re-doing the field. I am resetting the hedge. Do not move quickly in the plucking up. Many of the root systems that I have are entwined with evil systems that must gently be removed. Turn your face to the fire. You have tried to run and leave the fire. Turn your face to the fire and watch the burning and clearing for the wind of My Spirit is in the fire this hour. I must send forth the burning so there will not be an evil root left. For those who fear My name, I will rise over you as the sun of righteousness. That is where your shade will come forth. I will rise again, so turn your face to the fire. Face the wind of the fire and in the midst of the cleansing, I will rise again.

"Turn your face to the fire and receive your health. Turn your face to the fire and receive your cure. Turn your face to the fire and deliverance will come. My refreshing is in this fire. The sun of righteousness will rise over you and you will stand in the land with a new stand. The healing in My wings will restore your fields. Turn your face to the fire in your field and watch Me burn away that which would keep you from moving under My wing of healing. Don't resist the burning of the field. Turn your face to the fire for that is where you will be healed. Many snakes have been in your field and by the cleansing of the field the snakes will be seen and will leave your field. Turn your face to the fire and My peace will rise up in you. I am in a repair mode and I must burn away and remove so I can repair. Turn your face to the fire and I will repair your broken wing."

Keep turning until you have turned into the new path ahead. Do not let the enemy wear you down. Daniel wrote:

> *Until the Ancient of Days came, and judgment was given to the saints of the Most High [God], and the time came when the saints possessed the kingdom.... But the judgment shall be set [by the court of the Most High], and they shall take away his dominion to consume it [gradually] and to destroy it [suddenly] in the end. And the kingdom and the dominion and the greatness of the kingdom under the whole heavens shall be given to the people of the saints of the Most High; His kingdom is an everlasting kingdom, and all the dominions shall serve and obey Him* (Daniel 7:22, 26-27 AMP).

The Lord began to show me that He is taking us back to the blessing of the root. That is why some of you are not seeing the blessing you need to see. You need to go back to the blessing of the root! We will not just look at the top or appearance of a thing, but will look at the root. The love of money is the root of all evil. Ask the Lord to deliver you from the root of the love of money. Ask Him to restore any root system that has been overtaken by darkness. Ask Him to dig around, fertilize, and water the seeds that are deep within you. Ask for Him to strengthen what remains. Do not grow weary! You will triumph in the midst of the changing trends ahead! Pray in such a way that you receive revelation for the battle and live in such a way that you withstand the schemes of the enemy!

In the previous chapters, we've spotlighted the trends we've seen in the Church. Now, in the closing chapters, we want to look at how the Lord helps us to enter a new level of faith as new wineskins change and shift and we learn how to process the trends and changes occurring in the Church.

Endnotes

1. January 8, 2006, USGAPN Leadership Meeting, Denton, TX.

2. These enemies include: Dampness, Robbers, Intruders, Little Foxes, Moochers, Different Kinds of Seed being Sown, Decay, Waste, and finally, Jezebel and Ahab.

Chapter 16

A Time of Changing Structures
BY CHUCK D. PIERCE

*There comes a time
when wineskins or structures change!*

When reading through the Book of Matthew, we find the ministry of John the Baptist defining a wineskin. That definition would be altered by the ministry of Jesus. After Jesus was initiated into ministry through John's baptism and spent 40 days in the desert wilderness, He received a new baptism. He was led into the wilderness by the Spirit and came out with power!

Jesus then began forming *His* wineskin. Only Andrew, who came from John the Baptist's wineskin, made the shift to the new structure. In Matthew 11, John became disillusioned in prison, and asked his disciples to find out if Jesus, the Messiah, the One he baptized, was really the One they were hoping for. In Matthew 14, John was beheaded. The new wineskin was forced to accelerate. By this time, John's disciples had either realigned with the Pharisees (see Matt. 9:14) or were seeking the new baptism.

The Lord has a day for a structure that has been in place to make a shift. I believe the Ruler of Heaven, the King of kings, initiates these changes in the earth. Psalms 24:1 says, *"The earth is the Lord's and the fullness thereof!"* He is still the same, yesterday, today, and forever, so He knows when He is ready to take His Church into a new realm of understanding His goodness and love. He is, after all, sovereign in the aspect of timing and change.

He must create new structures for His plan of fullness. He also knows the structure that is necessary to accommodate and produce His plan in the earth. He looks at how we have been operating in the earth in one form or measure and says, "I must enlarge you and that which I have given you to steward, so I can express Myself in new ways."

Become Large Enough to Receive His Fullness

Fullness is a time word. For something to come to fullness, you must have a structure or container to fill. The earth is the Lord's. That is His container to fill with His glory. However, from generation to generation, He must create different types of structures to assist Him in pouring out this glory. Fullness means:

- *He fills until we run over! He fills until His plan is fulfilled* (see John 1:16). The Spirit of God does not just fill to the brim. He fills until the structure runs over, pours out, and covers the place assigned.

- *There is a place of abundance* (see John 10:10). There is a place that this filling and pouring occur. Look around your place and see if things are filling up with His glory.

- *In Him, we move and have our being* (see Acts 17:24-28; Col. 1:19; 2:9). Fullness is linked with life. Life means movement. The fuller we are with His Spirit, the better we move.

~ *He needs something that He can fill up or bring to completion* (see Matt. 9:16; Mark 2:21; 6:43; 8:20). The concept of fullness has to have a vessel.

~ *The salvation of the Gentiles has come into a number that satisfies God's requirement for completeness* (see Rom. 11:12,25). God loves people. He created Israel and the Jews. He is the God of Israel. In the Jews' rejection of the Messiah, a door opened for salvation to come to the Gentiles. His plan of fullness is now working to bring the salvation of the Gentile and Jew into overflowing.

The measure of Christ's blessing can overflow in us (see Rom. 15:29), in the earth, and in time (see Eph. 1:10; Gal. 4:4). God's sovereign appointment of events in our time is linked with His plan to restore and produce fullness. His Divine nature maturing in us is linked to His plan of fullness (see Col. 2:9). His love is so deep for us that we cannot measure it in terms of the world's measurement methods (see Eph. 3:18-19). His plan of fullness is linked with His visitation from generation to generation.

His Fullness: Linked With a Structure or Wineskin

As believers mature in their faith, they come into unity with Him. For this to occur, His government must be established. Therefore, the development of the way we think and the type of structure that holds and manifests that thinking process is linked with His plan of fullness in the earth! When Jesus was ascending to the right hand of Father God to make Himself available to us in this age, He gave gifts. He knew that we would have to allow gifts to develop in the earth that could govern the earth.

I believe we choose what type of change we wish to receive. The change is offered, but we must choose. At the end of 2008, I believe we entered the year of a new wineskin! Just as we have seen the United States of America shift to the next wineskin in civil government, we are seeing the Church make a shift in its thinking.

The word *new* is an interesting word. In *Interpreting the Times*, I discuss how to receive the new. (I hope you will read that book as well. It will really help you to process the new season we have entered.) I shared:

> The goal we should have in each of our transitions of life is to make it from the ending of one season into the beginning of the next new season. The word *new* can mean something that has never been or existed before. However, new is usually defined as "different from one of the same which existed before, something stale that has been made fresh, or something of one quality that has advanced into a better quality."[1]

Resisting God's Structures

Matthew 9:16 is a great example of Jesus teaching about the new. He addressed John's disciples and the Pharisees by using an analogy of a wineskin. These two groups were the two spiritual wineskins. These old wineskins were accusing Him over why His disciples were not being required to exercise the spiritual discipline of fasting the way they had fasted in the past. Jesus essentially said, "We are not going to do it the old way with the same old methods that have worked in the past!" He then said, "You cannot put new wine in an old wineskin!" (See Matthew 9:17.)

In other words, there needed to be a better quality skin developed to receive what was going to be poured out during the three years in which Jesus would walk with His disciples. He said, and I paraphrase, "If the new goes in the old, you will lose the old and the new. Let's preserve what has gotten us to this point. However, let's develop a new quality structure to hold the revelation that will be the fuel for us to advance."

John the Baptist's disciples did not want to make this shift into the new season. They had developed an order in how they were paving the way for the Messiah to come. They would give a call to the people of the land and then lead them out into a wilderness place. This place near the Jordan River would become the "place of the scapegoat." John would preach repentance and turning from sins. He used language like, "You vipers, you snakes, turn now!" As they named their sins in the wilderness, they would then be baptized. This was the way of salvation for the time leading up to Jesus.

Even Jesus went out to the wilderness to be baptized. Only Andrew left John in the wilderness and followed Jesus into the cities to eat with publicans and sinners. John was not excited about the changes that were coming to Israel through Jesus, the One for whom he had prayed, interceded, and paved the way. To embrace a new wineskin, you must let go and quit clinging to the familiar. Matter of fact, if you hold on to the last structure, you will be limited in how you can grow, mature, and efficiently operate in time in your place of stewardship. Here are some of the areas or old structures to which we cling:

- ∞ Our Thought Processes—we need a new *mindskin*
- ∞ Old Methods—some are good, some are bad

- Yesterday's Message—great revelation, but not relevant today

- A Narrow Form—one that was pliable in the past season, but is now becoming rigid

- Established Markets—creative products for a time, but now new innovation is required

- A Great Glory Manifestation—this created belief and reorganized your life, but now God is moving in a new way that is stretching you again

- A Lesser Power and Demonstration—He has more to show us

Jesus moved His disciples into a new season with His teaching and example. He raised a 12-year-old girl from the dead. As He moved forward to reach this young girl, a woman who had been ill with an issue of blood for 12 years pressed through the crowd to touch Him. He released His virtue, and she was immediately healed.

What can we learn from this? Remember that time is significant here, so we first look at the 12 years. Twelve is a number representing a new administration. Twelve is the number representing the apostolic gift. The next generation or administration lay dormant (represented by the young girl), whereas the old administration was pressing through (represented by the woman).

When Jesus determines to move into the new, then we who are being taught by Him must choose to respond. Representing the last season, the woman with the issue of blood had to press past her gender issue (she was a woman). She had to press past the law that barred anyone with an issue of blood from the public. There will always be a crowd that one must press through. But she was desperate, and the Lord acknowledged her and delivered her from her past season and its conflicting religious structure. As we press and touch in our desperation, we begin our next season of new life.

Jarius' young daughter represented the next administration. When Jesus reached her, He said, *"...she is not dead, but sleeping"* (Luke 8:52 NKJV). After removing the wailers from the room, He commanded her to arise! The next administration awakened. Remember that the grief of one season must end in order for you to awaken to the next season.

If you are moving in the new, you will see several changes occur in you: His fullness will be seen in your personality. Your soul will be restored from the last season. All fear and manipulation that have crowded your identity and confined you to your past will leave your personality. Your new identity will reflect His ability to overcome the mountains in the past season that stopped your progress. (See Isaiah 41 and Zechariah 4.)

He has given you power over your enemies who would hinder your progress (see 2 Cor. 10:3-6).

A Peculiar People, Holy Spirit Empowered

Remember, we are a people who comprise a nation that is above all nations. However, concerning the governments of this world, we are called to pray for all of those in authority, not just for those whom we prefer to win elections. We are a "peculiar people," not a political caucus. We are a people who can steer the course of history with our prayers and acts of faith. Jesus had to deal with the mind-set of some of His key leadership who were more interested in making Him a king of a nation than in recognizing Him as King of the Kingdom of God.

We must rely on the Holy Spirit as we enter a new season. The Holy Spirit must become our rear guard as we advance. Unless the Holy Spirit continues to be enfolded into the history of any land and continues directing its covenant with God, evil will overtake the society, causing our covenant root with our Creator to wither.

The Holy Spirit enables us to triumph as we go through great change. As we approach the future, the real issue always concerns the change of heart and unified expression of His people, which will release an anointing throughout the earth. The anointing breaks the yoke! (See Isaiah 10:27.) God always has a triumphant reserve from generation to generation that will come forth with new strength and power.

The way we think and the ways in which our minds align with God's mind are key. This is what we will discuss in the next chapter—how to enter a new season of critical thinking as we align our thoughts with God's thoughts.

ENDNOTE

1. Chuck D. Pierce, *Interpreting the Times* (Lake Mary, FL: Charisma House, 2008), 154.

Chapter 17

The New Season of Focused Critical Thinking

BY CHUCK D. PIERCE

~~~~~~~~~~~~~~~~~~~~~~~~~~~~~~~

Aligning our thoughts with God's thoughts

Changing our minds and realigning our thoughts is a process we all go through when we simplify our lives. After illness touched me, I had to change my way of thinking and begin to carry the burden and the prophetic insight the Lord had given me in a new way. I had to learn to "pause"—even in the midst of the crisis that I had been called to intercede through—and take the time for some much-needed rest and refreshment of body, soul, and spirit.

The Lord is doing so much with all of us during this season. That makes it vitally important for us to simplify, streamline, and think as He does if we are to accomplish the exploits He has planned for us. I believe His main goal is for us to understand His mind as we enter the next level of promise in the land He has given each of us to possess. You and I have an inheritance, yet many things can get in our way. Religious strongholds form and have authority to work within our thinking processes when we refuse to connect our thoughts properly. Jesus told us that you cannot patch an old quilt with new material and you cannot pour new revelation into an old structure. In approaching the new, we must dismantle the old. We must dismantle our old thought processes very precisely and build new ways of critical thinking. New connecting ideas of time, season, action, and methods must align in our thinking processes.

This entails the tearing down of strongholds that resist our sphere and try to keep our field from producing a new crop. I write about this in *The Future War of the Church*.[1] When a new thought has a hard time connecting with your existing stored thought structure in order to creatively develop a new way of doing things, you most likely have a stronghold. A stronghold is a thought process that is resistant to the will of God. This thought process gets impregnated by a demonic force and causes you to resist aligning your mind with the mind of Christ.

We all process what we see and feel from using our senses, but we do not all process information or revelation in the same way. If you are not careful, you can reject someone because they see things from a different perspective than you do. Cultures and races process information differently. Your environment influences your thoughts. Genders can process what they see and how they perceive something very differently; a man and a woman can look at the same object or seascape or mountain and describe what they see totally differently.

However, "in Him" we should all come up with the ultimate will of the One who created us; we should all know Him when we see Him. Key to our success is the way in which we process and grab hold of the perfect, acceptable will of God in the midst of a world filled with distractions. Distractions can cloud decision-making and discernment.

To be successful for the future, we need to filter out those distractions and choose the best way to proceed.

You start each day with a thought. Capture that thought. Keep things simple as you process the impression you receive from the One who knows best how to order your day. Romans 6:14 (NKJV) says, *"For sin shall not have dominion over you, for you are not under law but under grace."* Is there an area in your life that has dominion or rulership over you in your thoughts? This is how you detect a stronghold. The thought process linked with this stronghold must be dismantled.

Be aware that such strongholds may form around an emotion in you that has been wounded; often what you are doing or "acting out" is an attempt to mask the real emotional hurt. Ask the Lord for the grace to overcome. Know that you can triumph over the condemning cycle of thought that tries to overrule you. Romans 8:6-8 (NKJV) says:

> *For to be carnally minded is death, but to be spiritually minded is life and peace. Because the carnal mind is enmity against God; for it is not subject to the law of God, nor indeed can be. So then, those who are in the flesh cannot please God* (Romans 8:6-8 NKJV).

Steps Toward Critical Thinking

The Lord asks us questions to cause us to think differently and critically. He stirs our minds and prompts us so that we will seek His way. So think differently. Watch your prayer life change as you dialogue with the Lord in a new and different way each day. As I examine the teachings and ministry of Jesus, I find it interesting that He, having all knowledge as the Son of God, still chose to ask us questions rather than just supply all the answers for us. He stirs our hearts and minds by asking a question echoed in Matthew 16:15: *"Who do you say that I am?"*

Even today, God still demands a response to each question He asks and to each thought we have that exalts our way of thinking above His. This is what makes God so real—the Lord has never ceased interacting with His people. As we interact with Him, we can begin to tear down strongholds and develop our identity for the future. He desires a people who are willing to gather His thoughts, assess His ways, and then align with His strategies. That is the essence of critical thinking for the astute believer: aligning with God's thoughts.

Dismantle Strongholds!

To dismantle strongholds and align with God's thoughts, we must go through the process of realigning the way we think. Each of us can take some steps to accomplish this. Following are a few steps you can take to sharpen your mind, develop critical thinking skills, and capture your thoughts. Contrary to popular belief, you can teach an old dog new tricks. I am living proof of this! Recently the Lord visited me while I was in my office preparing to speak at our church's Feast of the Tabernacles celebration. He said, "In these critical times, you must think critically."

That statement left a profound mark on me. I knew a few things about the process of critical thinking. However, the Lord intended to teach me about it in new depth.

I believe each of us has the ability to learn how to think differently. Each of us is a "gifted and talented" child in God's Kingdom. You and I can come up with the answers to difficult questions. We do not have to have every answer ready today in this changing world. Part of our anxiety comes from not knowing or understanding hard questions in life. However, we can think the way He thinks. If we trust in our own knowledge, we will miss the mark. But we can be in harmony with Him and have our thoughts aligned with His; then our spirits will bear witness to His Spirit of life.

One step to take in thinking critically and aligning with God's thoughts is to heed the checks. That means using some discernment as we perceive challenges ahead and decide how to meet them. A godly imagination is key for us to walk in creativity; yet, if we do not bring our imaginations into alignment with God's perspective in any situation, we could allow our carnal minds to rule our emotions.

Anxiety can be triggered by anything that causes our spirit man to be alarmed. This is a good thing in the sense of being aware of dangers or challenges ahead. However, when we perceive a challenge ahead, if we do not process our thoughts correctly, we can create friction internally and eventually damage our whole being. To meet a challenge and carry the burden of it properly, we need to "heed these checks." How we process and carry burdens as they come into our lives will determine our long-term ability to overcome.

We Must Be Discerning

Discernment comes in two ways: by the Spirit and by the Word. Each time we develop a greater understanding of the Word, we can discern the world around us more sharply. Discernment means that we will rightly divide the complexity of the events around us and choose the best way to advance. Discernment and faith work hand in hand. Continuous exercising of faith causes you to come to full age or maturity. You learn to divide between sound and unsound stimuli. This allows you to act with proper conduct and avoid misconduct on your path of life. You will hear a word from behind you (see Isa. 30:21) or a grip inside of you. Heed that voice and obey.

Discipline Yourself

Another step toward thinking critically is to discipline yourself so that you can focus. I have sat in many think tanks where creative ideas were flying right, left, under the table, and swirling above my head. In the midst of that creative activity, I have found I must capture the one thought I need and focus on that wisdom. Again, it involves discernment and alignment to think the way God thinks about things.

I have chosen the Bible as the absolute authority that shapes my entire belief system and the way I think. Many people adhere to the principles of the Bible, but the Bible is far more than principles—it is the Word of life! The Bible is a living book that helps us understand the existence of God. Yet not only can we get to know God through the Word, we can also hear Him. His Holy Spirit speaks to us directly through His living, active words. This is the foundation for our thinking.

With such a foundation, we are able to answer every question we are ever asked based upon this living book. We can approach problems differently based upon how we see God approach problems in Scripture. Even the ultimate question of why we exist is answered in our relationship to a loving God in pursuit of us, which is displayed throughout Scripture.

Through basing our beliefs upon the Word, we can agree with Hebrews 11:3:

> *By faith we understand that the worlds [during the successive ages] were framed (fashioned, put in order, and equipped for their intended purpose) by the word of God, so that what we see was not made out of things which are visible* (AMP).

No matter how critical things become, we can be a people who can think the way God thinks and see our way into victory.

The key requirement for His new wineskin is this: become a critical thinker.

Each year, I look at the time we are living in from a Hebraic perspective. For instance, each year has a specific meaning that helps us think properly. In 2009, the year was "Tasting and Seeing the Lord's Goodness." To *taste and see* means that we must discern at a new level. In 2010, we have entered the season of *Ayin* (His eye will guide). Each year ends a season and begins a new season. That forces us into a time of transition. With every transition, our minds have to develop new thoughts. We go through deaths and measures of confusion until we finally start seeing our new ways of thinking develop and manifest.

For every process of moving into a new dimension, change is necessary. Mind-sets have to be altered. Old patterns must make way for new ones. As warriors called by God, we contend with the enemies of our time that seek to thwart any advancement of God's Kingdom. As we unfold God's battle plan for these days, we can apply divine strategy to enforce the victory. To become the Triumphant Reserve (a remnant that is held for "such a time as this") that we are called to be for this hour and to represent a holy God in this age, we must take the steps I have outlined to move into a new dimension of critical thinking.

A critical thinker processes information through a system of filters. As believers, our primary filter should always be the Holy Spirit, who testifies to and perfectly aligns with the written Word of God. Other filters include our own experiences, feelings, memories, intuition, and insights gathered from the past. Thinking critically involves keeping both an open mind to new revelation and adhering to the established safeguards of the mind, all of which have been constructed throughout our years of living.

When you think critically, you take in information, carefully evaluate its purpose, and reflectively relate the information to realign your emotional inner being. This improves your judgment. When you critically evaluate something, you develop vital questions, gather, assess, and interpret the information, and then come to well-reasoned conclusions and solutions.

However, in God's Kingdom, you do not rely upon your own understanding to do all this. Rather, you allow the Spirit of God to reveal hidden meanings in situations and challenges that will cause you to know God and His destined purposes. You do not look on the outward appearance of things; your view goes deeper, into the inner meaning of the spiritual force behind what you are seeing. This new perspective will cause you to see God's solution as opposed to your own.

The people of God must develop critical thinking to proceed into the days ahead. It is an indispensable quality. People must be able to hear the Lord as He asks them vital questions that will change the way they think. It is through critical thinking that the Lord will download key strategies to His people. Therefore, the Body of Christ must have the ability to evaluate the relevant data coming from God as He speaks to us from the Word, from revelation, and from events in the earth. We must spend time reaching godly, reasoned conclusions about these days and then take the appropriate actions to alter course. The Church must display excellent judgment in this hour. In the Old Testament, it was said that the sons of Issachar *"had understanding of the times, to know what Israel ought to do"* (1 Chron. 12:32 NKJV). So must God's people know the times and understand what to do today.

Meditation: The Key to Success!

Meditation on God's Word is another vital step toward critical thinking. I used to think I had to read eight chapters of the Bible a day to be spiritual. However, I came to a very simple conclusion: If I meditate upon even one verse and then am able to recite that Word from memory, it would become part of my being. Meditation causes us to chew the Word until our thoughts realign with God's, almost as a cow chews the cud until the nutrients of that fodder become part of its life.

When we meditate, we reflect, moan, ponder. This is a mental exercise where we quietly repeat out loud what we are thinking on. In our case, we are thinking on the Word of God. From this, we become united in communion with the One who created us for worship. Meditation is like a cow "chewing her cud." She has four stomachs and she begins the process by chewing, swallowing, regurgitating. Then she repeats this four times until what she is eating is now in her blood, producing milk for her children, and also giving her strength for the days ahead. This is meditation.

After meditating on the Word, we are to watch until the situation arises in which we put that Word into action.

Train Your Brain for the New!

I have provided some Scriptures for you to meditate on that will help you develop critical thinking skills. At the end of each verse, I provide some questions to help you develop a new way of critically thinking. Meditate on these questions. Let the Spirit of God penetrate your thinking processes with the Word and penetrate your emotions with the questions. This is a time to adopt critical thinking methods in our leadership and personal strategies so that we overcome and advance into the season ahead.

Some have asked me how I prophesy at the level I do, with the complexity and the intricate revelation brought forth from time to time. I meditate on many versions of the Bible. I encourage you to use whatever Bible version you are most comfortable with.

As an example, I have compiled the verses from various versions to show you the richness and varied thought processes you can develop as you read the Word from different perspectives (see Appendix B).

Here is a key question to ask yourself at the end of the day: Am I filled with joy and rejoicing over the decisions I made, no matter how hard they were?

Steps to Spiritual Creativity

Unlock the creative genius hidden in you. I think we have misunderstood the word *genius*. Therefore, we limit this category to those with exceptionally high IQs. Yet intelligence is not just linked to a high IQ. Our environment and genes play an important part in what makes us think and act the way we do. Generational iniquity can rob a person of his or her ability to think and act efficiently and effectively.

Intelligence is developed in someone who is willing to overcome the spirit of fear and insecurity and break new ground. This type of adventurist will uncover what has been hidden. This results in discoveries, witty inventions, and magnificent and new artistic displays. This type of creativity changes the way people view the world, field, or sphere where they are working. People with genius capacity will use their intelligence in a productive or impressive way. Their brain is functioning and agile. They do not overlook information or stimuli that others consider irrelevant.

In *New Thinking for a New Season!*, Sharon King writes the following:

> The brain is the machinery of the mind and these are clearly the days we need our brains regenerated to accommodate new ways of thinking, feeling and doing. We have a saying in Neurology, "Cells that fire together, wire together." This statement means that our experience literally wires our brain. If two neurons (brain cells) are connected and are electrically active at the same time, the connection between them gets stronger but if they are not electrically active together then those connection points called synapses are pruned or lost. To think in a new way, we need to have new electrical pathways formed in our brains; old ones cannot be remolded! This is the new wine in an old wineskin

scenario that Jesus talks about in Matthew 9. We need to activate new firing to get new wiring in our brain connections![2]

Our old, cluttered thoughts can be a hindrance to how we process a new way of doing things. I think this is one of the reasons we go through many of the issues we go through in life. Mainly, the Lord has a better way for us to do things, and we resist submitting to the changes that will make life better.

The old will always war with the new. There will always be problems waiting for answers. Here are some suggestions and an order of cognitive processing that I have developed to streamline my thinking and solve problems in my life:

Define your problem and clarify your real concern. What is your bottom-line issue? Evaluate all information you have about how you got into the mode of thinking that seems to have captured your freedom. Get some help to pinpoint the missing pieces that keep you from thinking in full, complete thoughts. Notice if you halfway complete sentences when you communicate or if you do not fully think through a problem, and address these issues.

Define your traps. Ask the Spirit of God to reveal your biases. Clarify your position and how much authority you have in the situation confronting you. Identify root causes of the problem that you are addressing. Do not let the surface fruit of the problem keep you from seeing the source that is feeding and producing the conflict.

Determine what point of view you are using in your analysis. Be willing to shift your perspective at any time. Ask yourself, "Am I limiting my thought processes to only what I know?" (Limited thought processes are synonymous with self-righteousness.)

Identify anything that you are taking for granted in your analysis. Do not allow your assumptions to cause you to look foolish.

Check to make sure you are not making intellectual judgments based on partial truths.

Ask yourself, "Have I simplified things to the point that I'm missing out on a major component?" Avoid bias or prejudice in the way you receive, perceive, and release information. Be willing to repent and change your mind. Ask forgiveness where appropriate. Be cleansed. Receive grace and ask for your mind to be healed.

In these changing times, you can succeed. Whatever you place your hand on can prosper. The way we think reflects in our work, our building processes, our vision, and our identity. Thinking critically in every new season determines the trends for that season. You are called to be part of the head and not the tail at setting the course for the future. Be connected to His Headship and your head will be "put on straight" to lead in God's Kingdom plan in the days ahead.

Endnotes

1. Chuck Pierce, *The Future War of the Church* (Ventura, CA: Regal Books, 2001).

2. Sharon King, *New Thinking for a New Season!* (Book currently in manuscript form).

Chapter 18

Prepare for the Next Season
BY CHUCK D. PIERCE

*The Lord reveals what we need to move
from one age to another.*

Yes! I believe the Lord will reveal anything we need to know in order to move from one age to another, according to His divine plan.

We have been given the written Word that can come alive in our age. The Holy Spirit dwells in the earth to teach, comfort, convict us when we stray from God's best, and judge the works of the enemy who would attempt to ensnare us on any given day. We are a people submitted to the King who rules a perfect Kingdom. He does nothing without first announcing His plans to the prophets who interpret His Word for such a time as this.

On May 31, 2008, I was ministering at a major gate of this nation in Liberty Park, New Jersey. As the spirit of prophecy began to fall, I exclaimed what our nation would look like in the future. I have not yet had the liberty to discuss all that I saw. However, I will say that the Lord showed me, first of all, my own bloodline's history in this land. He then showed me each state. He showed me the rapidly changing covenant alignment of each state of the nation of the United States of America. Some states were diverting from His purposes and developing laws and entering into time frames that opposed His covenant plan. Each state had thrones contending for the future.

Several months later, in October 2008, I met my wife, Pam, and some of my children at the Grand Canyon. The Grand Canyon is one of the natural wonders of the world. While we were at one of the incredible viewpoints on the rim, the Lord reminded me of the gathering in New Jersey and spoke to me:

> "A new type of river is now rising in this land. This river will create a schism unlike anything this nation has ever known before. Be prepared, for this nation as you know it will no longer be the same. I have brought you into a season of the new wineskin. Tell My people to be prepared for structures to change. This nation [America] is a wineskin, and you must begin to notice how changes will now accelerate. You must gain momentum in My Kingdom plan, or else new Kingdom rules will overthrow you."

> I heard the Lord say, "That is the type of river that is coming. This river will become torrential and devastating to some and refreshing and moving to others, bringing you to a new place of harvest. Whichever way you process, the changes will determine how you are prepared for the future. You can choose to be on either side of the rift, or you can get in the river and travel to your next destination in the midst of the changing course of a land at this time!"

The key issue to remember in this season is that the river will create rifts. The river of God is stirring the fish but also cutting a new path for them to come into their place of habitation for the future. That means that the Church must change its structure and prepare for the river to run its course and bring a new supply of fish into our nets. Get your net mended and ready since times and seasons have changed. The Lord will fill our nets if we will creatively stand in the rising river and not fear.

Processing a Trend

I see many new trends entering our spheres of authority in days ahead. How does change come? In God's Kingdom, Heaven initiates the changes. There are blueprints in Heaven that are released and then we must reflect or build out of Heaven's plan. This blueprint develops deep within the heart of man from the heart of God. This creates new trends, administrations, and operations in the Body of Christ. We must remember that we unlock the Kingdom and we build the Church. This is another way of looking at the concept of wineskin.

A trend is linked with the concept of a general course change. This involves prevailing tendencies to cause a change in course. Think fashion! New trends create an industry. Another way of understanding a trend is to think *highway, road, river, coastline,* or the like. How the highway forms for travel is a trend. Recently I heard the Lord say this:

"Rise up! Let My atmosphere rise up around you and cut the ties necessary, so that I can cause you to fight again and be set into a changing wind. I am breaking down the old structure you've been protecting. It is you that has been protecting an old structure saying, 'Remake what I'm comfortable in.' I am breaking that down.

"Catch the changing wind of My Spirit, for you will land in a new place, in a new dimension of My Spirit. You will say, 'I see a new land and I'm leaving the winds from the wilderness.' You had expectations in some relationships that you're still trying to work out. I've been contending to cut you loose from those relationships. I am contending over you so that you rise up above the inordinate structure of the enemy that has been placed around you. Get ready to rise up, for I am contending and My sword is the strongest. Raise your sails and catch the wind. You have been in a dry and desolate land. But even though water has not been there for you to move forward, I will send the water if you will raise the sail.

"This is a time to know My presence. This is a time to know My ark and to know what ark you are to enter to journey into your future. I am causing My presence to flood in the land. Raise your sail and watch the glory begin to take you to a new place. Don't hesitate. Hesitation is set as a snare to My movement for your life. Let your faith push you and catapult you. When you hear the wind of truth being spoken into a situation, move immediately. You don't want to miss the boat. You don't want to miss your proper alignment. Don't hesitate. Delay is set as a trap. The Word is critical in this hour. The intensity that is behind the Word is pushing you forward at speeds and levels that

we know not of, so don't hesitate and don't fall for the trap.

"Within the sands of your desert, there is a highway. But in the sands of your desert you have grown accustomed to the atmosphere and the sirocco wind that has been around you. In the sands of your desert, create a new atmosphere and I will cause that highway that is down deep to rise up. For there are ways of escape for My people in this next season. There are ways of escape that are forming, but you must create the wind that causes the highway to rise in front of you. I am laying the road. I am laying a road. Watch it form now. Go with Me on this new road, for you are headed into a place that you have not been. You must bring forth the wind and create the road so that you can end up where I have called you to be—new businesses, new alignments, new assignments.

"I'm having you return to some business associates that you separated from and chose to walk a different direction from in this past season. Even now, you will go back and re-form a new way to venture forward. New ventures are on the horizon for My people. You must now grab hold and get on a highway that sets you ahead of the curve. You will go back and re-form a plan with them like Paul went back and got John Mark. These relationships will no longer be the same, but will be brought under a new covenant plan. They were once in an old structure, but now will be brought into a new structure. If those relationships are unwilling to come into a new structure, move on down the road

for there are new relationships that will create this new venture. I will give some opportunities that did not manifest in the past season and now they will have an opportunity for a manifestation in this season. The ventures of My people now will take a shift in their formation. Realign and then align again so that those ventures might manifest properly!"

The ancient definition of *trend* is aligned with the word *"to trundle"* or *"to run."*[1] These are thought patterns that produce methods and create new administrations that stretch us from one direction toward a different direction. Another definition of trend involves the part of a stock of an anchor.[2] The trend portion determines the size of the anchor. That portion is relegated to how large a ship you can make stationary in the future. A trundle is any round body or circle that produces a throne and a type of knowledge.[3] If you think of a trundle bed, it is one that you roll under another bed. It doesn't become the foundation of that bed, but becomes the accessory necessary to complete the process of that room.

Another way to think of a trend is the concept of a stepladder. When you embrace one rung of change, it produces the next step to take you to a higher place.

Receive the new! The new shift produces shaking!

There comes a time when you leave a transition and shift into the new. No longer can you keep prophesying that the new will happen. There comes a time when the new happens. At that moment, our whole being must make a shift. We may have some difficulties shifting into a new season, so I feel we should define the word *shift*.

To shift is to "change the place, position, or direction of."[4] A shift reflects these changes and also includes an exchange or replacement of one thing for another. A shift is a change of gear so you can accelerate. A shift can also be an underhanded or deceitful scheme. Therefore, in our shift we must recognize that the enemy is plotting to stop it. A shift also entails a scheduled time.

When a shift in trends occurs, the shaking begins. The Lord shakes loose our legalistic thinking processes that we have formed in the past season. Most Christians would be greatly surprised to learn how many legalistic structures they have embraced. Simply put, legalism is narrowing all of our mind processes down to the point that we can't receive the mind of God. Rather than having a mind-set that is saturated in His grace and love, legalism is a mind-set that is steeped in man's judgment and control.

Our restoration cannot be released while God is tightly locked in a box. He shakes loose condemnation. Satan is a liar and a thief. The Spirit of God shakes loose lies. Let the Holy Spirit soak you in His cleansing waters of forgiveness and renewal. This is another key to renewing the wineskin that will hold the wine of restoration. He shakes loose old judgments that formed in the past season. Isaiah 58 says that if you will pray and fast, and let God determine the fast for you (don't do it religiously), and if you'll put away the pointing of that finger and looking outward, He will begin to break forth your light and your healing will spring up. Let Him shake loose your healing!

A Timeline of Shaking

As I said earlier, much shaking occurs in shifting, trendsetting times. The prophet Haggai prophesied that

God would shake us until all the old mind-sets had been shaken from us. He would continue shaking until the *"The latter glory of this house will be greater than the former..."* (Hag. 2:9 NASB).

He shakes loose a new level of communion, vision, and relationship with Himself. He shakes loose our identity for the future. He shakes loose our ability to finish what we started. He shakes loose the ability for us to complete the projects we have begun.

For instance, the Lord showed me in January 1986 that by the end of January 1996, the government of God would begin to change. Then He showed me that by the end of 2006, His government would be in a new mature state. This meant that a new wineskin would be operating, and the way church had been done from 1966 to 2006 would come to an end. We are seeing this happen. I could document page after page of changes from various authors, but I believe anyone who reads this book will already know we are living in a different Church era. C. Peter Wagner has called it the "New Apostolic Reformation."[5]

The Lord showed me that by 2006, lawlessness would have many avenues of operation throughout the world. And indeed, we have seen lawlessness arise greatly. By 2016, in an effort to control this chaos, many laws will have been established that will severely restrict our freedom.

In *God's Unfolding Battle Plan*, I share the following:

Governments of the world cannot fully change until the government of God here on Earth aligns itself and represents the order of God. That means leaders in the Church must get their act together! I see many denominations or wineskins of the past fading and becoming irrelevant by 2016. There have already been many changes. We have become aware of God's foundational plan of apostles, prophets, evangelists, pastors and teachers. We are learning how to interact with each other. We are letting go of old methods of operation and embracing new ways of worship.

The real war in days ahead will come over how we fellowship. We will have to learn how to operate in decentralized fellowship. In other words, we won't all be going to church every Sunday. That form of worship is changing rapidly. At the same time, corporate worship gatherings in certain territories will break through into new levels of revelation. I am not talking about extra-biblical revelation— the Bible has been canonized; it is the established Word of God. However, I believe there is revelation coming that will cause the Word to become even more applicable for this age, while also giving us strategies to defeat the enemy. Many of what are now corporate warfare worship gatherings will turn into times of travail, and the result will be changed nations. As we come together and worship in such settings, we will gain new strategies for how to govern in our spheres of authority.[6]

ENDNOTES

1. Noah Webster's First Edition of an American Dictionary of the English Language (republished in facsimile edition by Foundation for American Christian Education, San Francisco, CA). Permission to reprint 1828 edition granted by G. & C. Merriam Company, copyright 1967, Rosalie J. Slater.

2. Ibid.

3. Ibid.

4. Merriam-Webster Online Dictionary, 2010, s.v. "shift," http://www.merriam-webster.com/dictionary/shift (accessed March 25, 2010).

5. C. Peter Wagner, *Churchquake! How the New Apostolic Reformation is Shaking Up the Church As We Know It* (Ventura, CA: Gospel Light 1999), 5.

6. Chuck D. Pierce, *God's Unfolding Battle Plan* (Ventura, CA: Regal Books, 2007), 24.

Chapter 19

Times of Restoration
BY CHUCK D. PIERCE

God takes what is there, makes us more flexible,
and brings us to new places
so He can release new wine in us.

When the Holy Spirit begins a process of restoration, He places us in a new season with new revelation and new life: a new wine. Most of us are familiar with the passage in Matthew 9:17 that says:

> *Nor do they put new wine into old wineskins, or else the wineskins break, the wine is spilled, and the wineskins are ruined. But they put new wine into new wineskins, and both are preserved* (Matthew 9:17 NKJV).

In order to contain the new wine of restoration, we need new wineskins. The Greek word for "new," meaning something totally new that has never been seen before, is *neos*. In Matthew 9:17, it is the word used to describe the wine.[1] Another Greek word is used in this passage in relation to the wineskins; that word is *kainos*, meaning something that has been renewed or made over—something restored.[2]

In the restorative process, God takes what was there and brings it to a new place so He can pour within it that which He longs to release to us—our new wine. To make a wineskin new, one must soak an old wineskin in water and rub it in oil. Rubbing in the oil is the part of the process that makes a wineskin flexible. Those hard things we go through are the oil that the Lord rubs into us. And that oil also contains a new anointing. As we allow the Holy Spirit to take us through the process of rubbing, we not only become more flexible so that we can handle all God desires to pour into us, but we also become able to pour out in a greater measure.

Beware: Jezebel Has a Plan!

We must get used to how God sees us. He calls us "The Triumphant Reserve"! This is a phrase that I want you to get used to. When the Lord caught me up into a realm of vision on May 31, 2008, at Liberty Park, New Jersey, the Spirit of the Lord showed me the timeframe in which He would work with this nation and other nations to produce fruit for the future. When I was looking down into the land, there were layers of darkness. I could see many areas, the glory realms of the earth that were captured by darkness. I saw how God would have to change entire structures before He could bring forth the harvest for the future. I could see evil root systems planted in the land. I could see evil root systems in my own bloodline based upon land structures that had never been dealt with.

The Lord said:

> My people are trying to manage their households and now I am going to have to cause the roots of the land to be pulled up and jarred. Therefore, you will again manage what I assign you, but this will be My time of uprooting. Allow Me to pull up evil structures. Manage what I am assigning you to manage while I am pulling up. Do not let your

pride try to stop Me from pulling things up and out that need to be pulled up.

As I mentioned earlier, this Triumphant Reserve was being held for *"a time such as this"* (see Esther 4:14). Many had been on shelves, waiting, but now they were being called forth. Others were realigning in new ways so they could war with their destined tribes. The Spirit of God was calling forth His troops for this hour. The Spirit of God showed me this Reserve and their strength and position in each state in America. He then took me higher and showed me the Reserve and their war for the future in the nations of the earth, God's inheritance. He honored me by giving me a glimpse of the 153 sheep nations in the earth that the angels were contending over. A sheep nation is one that has chosen to follow the Lord's covenant plan. All nations are eventually reconciled in their relationship around Israel. We find this in Ephesians 2:14-18.

Relieve the Weary! God Has a Reserve!

We have a large meeting each January to hear what the Lord has to say to us for the year ahead. In one of the meetings, I noticed something on the worship team. LeAnn Squier, who was sick during the conference, came as usual to the front line, but was limited in the strength she had to bring forth. John Dickson's voice began to struggle.

I heard the Lord say, "Relieve the front line." I called forth others from the back to come to the front and sing forth prophetically, even though this was not their normal role, and they responded. One person on the worship team began to pick up where another one was too tired to continue on. This became like a tag team. Weary ones stepped back for a while and others took their places. The power of revelation never ebbed again. Heaven remained connected in the earth realm and *"on earth, as it is in heaven"* (Matt. 6:10) kept occurring so we could walk victoriously throughout the year.

On the battlefield, many casualties can occur when troops get weary. Weariness can cause mental passivity, breakdowns, people going AWOL (Absent Without Leave), and even suicide and death. I believe the Lord is telling us to watch out for those who are exhausted and help them step back and get rejuvenated. He will call you to help someone so they can refocus for their victory ahead and not be taken out by the enemy. He will show you who you are to relieve in service, helps, and ministry.

The Enemy's Goal: Wear Down Your Mind!

In these days, we must remember Daniel's words:

As I looked, this horn made war with the saints and prevailed over them....And he shall speak words against the Most High [God] and shall wear out the saints of the Most High and think to change the time [of sacred feasts and holy days] and the law; and the saints shall be given into his hand for a time, two times, and half a time [three and one-half years] (Daniel 7:21,25 AMP).

The mind, heart, emotions, and well-being of the soul are intricately connected. Usually, the enemy's goal in persecution is not to "burn us at the stake." To persecute actually means to wear down your mind and remove your strength to disable you from having the right connected thought process for success and prosperity in days of turmoil. The heart thinks! Therefore, if the enemy can bombard you with thoughts that produce fear and anxiety, he can remove your ability to manifest the will of God in your life. The pure in heart see God. If our minds are weary and our hearts ache, then we lose the vision for the present and the future is captured. Do not allow the enemy to cause you to lose the focus of your inheritance. Your inheritance is your portion. This is your vineyard! The enemy is in war over the earth and the fullness thereof being the Lord's! (See Psalms 24:1.)

A Renewed Vineyard!

The Lord showed me the following principle as we began to study the vineyard. Every seven years, the vineyard was to lay fallow (see Exod. 23:11). According to the rabbis, the land, the workers, and the animals were to rest. The people were to study the Word during that seventh year.

This is a picture of dominion in the Messianic Kingdom! The seventh day Sabbath rest, the seventh year, the "seven times seven" creating a Jubilee, were all time sequences required for the new to manifest within God's people and His covenant plan. This is also a "new wineskin" principle. A wineskin could become new by being soaked in water and then oiled for seven years. Declare that you are becoming new—in quality, strength, and vision.

There were "rules of the vine" formed in the desert wilderness (see Deut. 6:11; Lev. 25:5-11). In the desert, the Lord gave Moses strategies and direction on how to prosper the vineyard. The fruit could not be eaten the first three years. The fourth year it had to be offered to the Lord. The fifth year the owner could *prosper* (see Mark 12:2). Judah's life adapted to the vine (see Gen. 49:11). As we move forward to see the Tabernacle of David restored, we must understand that the vine is being pruned. We must not be like the leaders who went into the Promised Land. These leaders, known as the spies, saw the bountiful, enormous clusters of grapes, cut them down, handled them, and tasted them, but would not go to war to possess the promise! (See Numbers 13.) Understanding the cluster of the grapes is a key to understanding the anointing.

We are being prepared! The preparation phase of the vineyard is the most costly. The vineyard must be enclosed in a permanent fence or hedge. The large stones in the field must be removed. Once removed by the husbandman, these stones were placed in rows. The rows of stones were used to train the vines how to trail. This protected the fruit from dampness. This pictures the stones that we remove from our lives. If we will use those besetting sins and wrong structures properly, they can be what cause the fruit in our lives to multiply.

A winepress had to be hewn out on location. This was done to prevent bruising of the fruit during transit. The proximity of the winepress near the ground of origination is important, also, because the taste and fullness of the grape was linked with that ground. The place that you have been called this hour is important!

Traditionally, two troughs were hewn parallel to each other, one higher than the other. The first trough was for *trodding*, the second was for *receiving* the juice. A *watchtower* was erected to watch and guard the vintage from thieves and jackals (see Isa. 5:1-7). The winepress was a place of triumph and overcoming. The vintage began in September with shouts of joy! People passing through had access to the grapes of the vineyard, but were forbidden to carry any away.

God is preparing us for the same type of overcoming experiential joy.

Endnotes

1. Biblesoft's New Exhaustive Strong's Numbers and Concordance with Expanded Greek-Hebrew Dictionary. CD-ROM. Biblesoft, Inc. and International Bible Translators, Inc. s.v. "neos," (NT 3501).

2. Ibid., s.v. "kainos," (NT 2537).

Where Evil Abounds, Grace Abounds Much More!

ↀↀↀↀↀↀↀↀↀↀↀↀↀↀↀↀↀↀↀↀↀ

Yes, there are great challenges confronting the Church in our day. But we have a great God! Regardless of the circumstances, God is good and has a plan for His Church and His Kingdom. It is just as the Scriptures say: *"…as people sinned more and more, God's wonderful grace became more abundant"* (Rom. 5:20).

As we remain broken before God, He gives us the power to overcome the failures we see in the Church world. We must look to Him to receive the new *mindskin* and out-of-the-box, innovative ways to impact the world for Jesus Christ. We have a divine responsibility to live like Him and proclaim Him with great power to our world.

The King of the Kingdom has a plan. As the Church, we have a Gospel to proclaim. The mission of the Church is to submit to Christ, and announce the good news to people in our neighborhoods and nations. The glorious news is that they can transfer their allegiance from the kingdom of this world to the Kingdom of Christ until *"The kingdom of the world has become the kingdom of our Lord and of His Christ…"* (Rev. 11:15 NIV).

There is a movement of spiritual renewal and revival going on in many places in our day. The possibilities of transformation flourish as we unite to truly become the Body of Christ. Let's seize the moment to affect the best of times for ourselves, our children, our families, the Church, and our future. May we press into Him, listen to His voice, and obey Him fully during these strategic days.

Operating Successfully in God's Kingdom Plan
BY CHUCK D. PIERCE

God has a plan for His Kingdom people.

God's Kingdom will increase from generation to generation. According to Luke 17:21, the Kingdom of God is within us. However, the Kingdom of God within us manifests in the earth. God has a plan of success for His Kingdom people. When we overcome and succeed in God's plan then we bring His fullness into the earth.

Here are "Ten Keys to Operating Successfully in God's Kingdom Plan":

1. *Be fruitful, multiply, and take dominion!* (See Genesis 1:28.) When God created us, He blew into us the ability to occupy and multiply. Break ties with any influencing structure that opposes this will.

2. *Understand the power of firstfruits!* (See Genesis 4:2-5; Proverbs 3:9-10; Matthew 6:33; Romans 11:16-18.) From Genesis to Revelation, the premise of *first* pervades the Word of God. Seek Him first and give Him the best first and all the rest will be blessed. Review your giving.

3. *Follow Him and He can determine your boundaries!* (See Genesis 11-12.) Promise and prosperity will manifest when we let go and *go!* Abraham followed and kept following until God made covenant with Him. Jesus taught His disciples to follow until they could become the apostles that would change the course of history.

4. *Bless the seed of Abraham and be blessed!* (See Genesis 12:3.) When we bless God's sovereignly chosen nation (Israel and His people, the Jews), we become blessed.

5. *Move in an aligned order and war for your inheritance!* (See Exodus 6:26; Numbers 10.) There is a defined order and alignment for your victory within your assigned boundaries, field, sphere, and market.

6. *Enter your boundaries and use your God-given power to "get wealth" and advance His covenant plan!* (See Deuteronomy 8.) He can give you the power to get wealth once you reevaluate your covenant purpose.

7. *Know your prophetic identity; receive favor; and occupy your sphere!* (See Genesis 49; Deuteronomy 33; Isaiah 45.)

8. *Listen to the prophets on how to succeed!* (See Second Chronicles 20.)

9. *Be a steward who multiplies!* (See Luke 19:11-27.) One area in which we are often judged involves stewardship: we are judged when we are given something to steward, but are afraid to take what we have been given and multiply it. You must look at all that you are holding in your hands as an assignment for multiplication and increase.

10. *Do exploits!* (See Daniel 11:32.) God will have a strong people in days ahead who take a resource and create other resources.

If you develop your mentality around these points, you will walk in a mind-set of victory.

Ten Trends for Today's Watchman

I am a watchman and try to watch carefully for patterns and trends that affect each of us. A watchman is one who peers into the future to see what is coming. Here are some things to watch for:

1. *The way the Church gathers and strategizes.* Several years ago God showed me a changing way of gathering that was occurring in His Kingdom plan. He revealed that new, faster, innovative ways of communication were coming. He showed me small, intimate gatherings in homes to strategize and gain direction to overcome in the world. He showed me our ability to meet, communicate quickly, and then advance and have influence in the world. He showed me the House Church Structure for the future and why this type of gathering in clusters was important. I wrote a foreword in Larry Kreider's book *House to House*. This book should be read by all. How we gather and strategize will be our key to overcoming in days ahead.

2. *How we worship in Spirit in truth.* We are living in a season of violence. We will triumph by becoming a "violent," (aggressively) praising people. The people of a new wineskin always sing their way into a new season before they theologically understand

the season. Our hearts must be impacted before our minds are informed. Before Scriptural trust is systematized, it is sung! (See Isaiah 42:10 and Colossians 3:16.) Triumphant songs of deliverance come forth and we break free through sound (see Exod. 15; Deut. 32; Rev. 15:3-4). These songs break atmospheric resistance, barrenness, and invasion of enemies. These triumphant songs of Heaven (see Rev. 5:9-10; 14:3; 15:3-4) break old cycles from past seasons that are holding us captive. Songs of victory and harvest will go before the changes that Heaven is bringing into the earth! (See Psalms 60.)

3. *Shifting, changing laws.* The enemy loves to change times and laws. Therefore, he will use worldly structures and controls to hinder Kingdom advancement. We must stay active in civil government. How we vote is how we are visited in the future. Politically motivated shifts in laws and governmentally influenced ventures and investments will produce blame and create power wars that divide and control certain institutions of societies.

4. *Changing supply lines.* Go back and review the gold market in every decade so you can find your pattern for the shift that will take place in currency in each season! *Money, economic regulations, and changing financial structures do not affect the Kingdom, but do affect how we build the Church in days ahead.* Unregulated derivatives will continue for a while longer. This will cause the banking system to change drastically and expand the supply of money and credit. This creates another bubble waiting to

burst. For instance, in the United States, individual states are losing revenue and beginning to cut services. The following are just some effects from these conditions: the poor will get poorer; there will be a decline in state workers; there will be cuts in medical services; there will be a lack of Medicare funding for the elderly; there will be a decline in education; there will be a greater potential for violence; there will be exhaustion of unemployment benefits.

5. *Slavery structures must be reviewed. Watch your debt structure!* Develop a plan for debt management and alleviation. Ask for favor with institutions. Notice governmental manipulation since July 2009. Many institutions will attempt to manipulate debt to make money. Debt produces poverty. We must watch debt patterns in our lives, counties, cities, and nations.

6. *Changing economic structures worldwide!* Inflation could happen at any time, so always have a plan for it. Consider your ways. Have plans to diversify your investments and resources. Do not put all of your eggs in one basket. Do not have a basket so "tight" that you cannot remove or add or redirect resources into Kingdom purposes and plans; your funds must not be so restricted that you cannot move in God's timing of shifts. For instance, keep watching and moving your natural resources, (gas and oil) to gold and silver stocks, at the appropriate timing. Watch the emerging markets of China and India. (I am sold on watching this!) Watch products that enhance the land such as fertilizer and other agriculture-related

ventures. Biotech developmental groups are always key for us to watch. His Kingdom is a sure thing in times of shifting economic trials.

7. *Restoration of waste places.* Carefully watch the cities where bulldozers begin to demolish old structures. Watch as the repairer of the breach calls us into a rebuilding season. Certain cities must be transformed.

8. *Realignment of nations.* Be aware of any "chess moves" made by Russia and China to counteract the U.S.-dollar base of world currency. This will affect many systems, but will fall short in complete governmental dominance and control. Israel will become more and more the center of discussion and division in nations in days ahead. China is attempting to create a new reserve currency. China is gathering and securing gold resources throughout the world. *The effect will be that a new world currency base is developing.*

9. *A major shift in training in God's Kingdom plan.* We must develop creative skills! We must become sensitive to the problems of people. We must address every obstacle as a challenge with an available solution. We must not fear causes because we know the Spirit can produce results through us. We must be motivated by a covenant expression of God's plan in the earth through His vision, rather than through money. We must be adaptable and observant to the changes around us. We must see the world around us differently, ask a lot of questions, and synthesize things from an intuitive perspective. We must become a fluent, flexible, and

imaginative people who are not afraid to be original and divergent in our thinking processes.

10. *Alignment and training for the future!* God has a battle array and an order that will reflect His holiness in days ahead. We will have a new vocabulary, a new presentation of identity, and a new dimension of authority as we enter the next season. New training structures are being developed to help God's people understand their covenant blessing and spiritual inheritance.

Do Not Back Up

You can move into a new place of divine revelation. You can understand and find the higher purposes in your circumstances and sufferings. Your captivity can become a place of rest. You can roar louder than the roaring lion seeking to devour you.

God is breathing praise on His people! Inhale His presence and then exhale His Spirit. He can redeem your past seasons of lost praise and your life will suddenly be restored. Your new identity will manifest and you will wear His boldness and be an answer in the world today.

Thought Processes to Develop:
Reading the Word
From Different Perspectives

BY CHUCK D. PIERCE

~~~~~~~~~~~~~~~~~~~~~~~~~~~~~~

A s you meditate on Scripture, consider reading a variety of versions, paying attention to the perspectives conveyed by each.

Be strong and very courageous. Be careful to obey all the instructions Moses gave you. Do not deviate from them, turning either to the right or to the left. Then you will be successful in everything you do. Study this Book of Instruction continually. Meditate on it day and night so you will be sure to obey everything written in it. Only then will you prosper and succeed in all you do. This is My command—be strong and courageous! Do not be afraid or discouraged. For the Lord your God is with you wherever you go (Joshua 1:7-9 NLT).

Give it everything you have, heart and soul. Make sure you carry out The Revelation that Moses commanded you, every bit of it. Don't get off track, either left or right, so as to make sure you get to where you're going. And don't for a minute let this Book of The Revelation be out of mind. Ponder and meditate on it day and night, making sure you practice everything written in it. Then you'll get where you're going; then you'll succeed. Haven't I commanded you? Strength! Courage! Don't be timid; don't get discouraged. God, your God, is with you every step you take (Joshua 1:7-9 MSG).

Ponder the following questions regarding Joshua 1:7-9:

∾ Do you understand the concept of success?

∾ Are you walking in a success mentality?

∾ Do you know where you are going?

∾ Are you pressing toward the manifestation of a promise in your life?

∾ Are your desires aligned with God's purposes?

∾ Do you feel as though you are on track right now?

∾ Has a mentor in your life imparted an unfulfilled promise for you to carry on to fullness?

I try to read one psalm each day. Meditate on Psalms 1:1-3:

Blessed is the man who walks not in the counsel of the ungodly, nor stands in the path of sinners, nor sits in the seat of the scornful. But his delight is in the law of the Lord, and in His law he meditates day and night. He shall be like a tree planted by the rivers of water, that brings forth its fruit in its season, whose leaf also shall not wither; and whatever he does shall prosper (NKJV).

How well God must like you—you don't hang out at Sin Saloon. You don't slink along Dead-End Road, you don't go to Smart-Mouth College. Instead, you thrill to God's Word, you chew on Scripture day and night. You're a tree replanted in Eden, bearing fresh fruit every month, never dropping a leaf, always in blossom (MSG).

How blessed are those who reject the advice of the wicked, don't stand on the way of sinners or sit where scoffers sit! Their delight is in Adonai's Torah; on His Torah they meditate day and night. They are like trees planted by streams—they bear their fruit in season, their leaves never wither, everything they do succeeds (CJB).

Here are some key questions on which to meditate for Psalms 1:1-3:

- Who are your closest associates?

- Who are your greatest influencers?

- Do you sense your mind thinking on the Word of the Lord throughout the day?

- Do you delight in the Word?

- Is the Word alive to you?

- Are you bearing fruit?

- Do you feel as though you are blossoming forth in the next level of identity for your life?

In this passage I attempt to show how you can associate Scripture prophetically from Old to New Testaments. Let's start with Proverbs 3:1-10:

My son, forget not my law or teaching, but let your heart keep my commandments; for length of days and years of a life [worth living] and tranquility [inward and outward and continuing through old age till death], these shall they add to you. Let not mercy and kindness [shutting out all hatred and selfishness] and truth [shutting out all deliberate hypocrisy or falsehood] forsake you; bind them about your neck, write them upon the tablet of your heart [see Col. 3:9-12]. So shall you find favor, good understanding, and high esteem in the sight [or judgment] of God and man [see Luke 2:52]. Lean on, trust in, and be confident in the Lord with all your heart and mind and do not rely on your own insight or understanding. In all your ways know, recognize, and acknowledge Him, and He will direct and make straight and plain your paths. Be not wise in your own eyes; reverently fear and worship the Lord and turn [entirely] away from evil [see Prov. 8:13]. It shall be health to your nerves and sinews, and marrow and moistening to your bones. Honor the Lord with your capital and sufficiency [from righteous labors] and with the firstfruits of all your income [see Deut. 26:2; Mal. 3:10; Luke 14:13-14]. So shall your storage places be filled with plenty, and your vats shall be overflowing with new wine [see Deut. 28:8] (AMP).

The Book of Proverbs changed my life. This question will direct your giving and health in days ahead:

- ∾ Do you understand the power of firstfruits—giving the Lord the best of the first?

- ∾ Do you have a nerve situation that needs healing?

- ∾ Do your barns need filling?

- ∾ Do you lean on your own way of thinking or do you wait for the Lord to show you the one thing that will change everything?

Do not fear changing. Meditate on the following selections from the Psalms 27:

> *The Lord is my light and the one who saves me. I fear no one. The Lord protects my life. I am afraid of no one. If an army surrounds me, I will not be afraid. If war breaks out, I will trust the Lord* (Psalms 27:1,3 NCV).

> *Wait and hope for and expect the Lord; be brave and of good courage and let your heart be stout and enduring. Yes, wait for and hope for and expect the Lord* (Psalms 27:14 AMP).

Answer these questions and quiet your emotions:

~ What is the number one fear in your life?

~ Do you fear warfare (spiritual and physical)?

~ Do you feel hope rising within you as you wait on the Lord, or would you classify your life as one that has been overcome and marked by hopes that have been deferred?

~ Are you expecting the Lord to move in a new way? Tell all fear to leave!

This is a season in which to be transformed. Memorize Romans 12:1-2:

> *I appeal to you therefore, brethren, and beg of you in view of [all] the mercies of God, to make a decisive dedication of your bodies [presenting all your members and faculties] as a living sacrifice, holy (devoted, consecrated) and well pleasing to God, which is your reasonable (rational, intelligent) service and spiritual worship. Do not be conformed to this world (this age), [fashioned after and adapted to its external, superficial*

> *customs], but be transformed (changed) by the [entire]*
> *renewal of your mind [by its new ideals and its new*
> *attitude], so that you may prove [for yourselves] what*
> *is the good and acceptable and perfect will of God, even*
> *the thing which is good and acceptable and perfect [in*
> *His sight for you]* (AMP).

Read, meditate on, memorize, and think on this Scripture as you answer these questions:

- ∞ Does a member of your body refuse to submit and become holy?

- ∞ Is there a particular worldly draw that keeps distracting and diverting you from being transformed to the will of God?

- ∞ Is the world fashioning you according to its blueprint?

Second Corinthians 10:3-6 will encourage you to capture your thoughts:

> *For although we do live in the world, we do not wage*
> *war in a worldly way; because the weapons we use to*
> *wage war are not worldly. On the contrary, they have*
> *God's power for demolishing strongholds. We demolish*
> *arguments and every arrogance that raises itself up*
> *against the knowledge of God; we take every thought*
> *captive and make it obey the Messiah. And when you*
> *have become completely obedient, then we will be ready*
> *to punish every act of disobedience* (CJB).

Ask yourself these questions:

- ∞ Am I exalting my thoughts above the Word of God in any area?

- ∞ Am I being arrogant in any area?

∾ Are my prideful insecurities keeping me from gaining the revelation and counsel I need for a new dimension of freedom?

Learn to keep your mind fixed. Meditate on the following selections from Isaiah 26:3-5:

People with their minds set on You, You keep completely whole, steady on their feet, because they keep at it and don't quit (Isaiah 26:3 MSG).

You will guard him and keep him in perfect and constant peace whose mind [both its inclination and its character] is stayed on You, because he commits himself to You, leans on You, and hopes confidently in You. So trust in the Lord (commit yourself to Him, lean on Him, hope confidently in Him) forever; for the Lord God is an everlasting Rock [the Rock of Ages] (Isaiah 26:3-4 AMP).

He humbles the proud and brings the haughty city to the dust; its walls come crashing down (Isaiah:26:5 TLB).

Answer the following questions:

∾ Do you have a hard time staying focused?

∾ Is there one area in your life that is keeping you from becoming whole (peace and wholeness being synonymous)?

∾ Does a stronghold need to be detected and broken in your life?

Let joy arise as you meditate on the following selections from Philippians 4:4-9:

Be full of joy in the Lord always. I will say again, be full of joy. Let everyone see that you are gentle and kind... (Philippians 4:4–5 NCV).

Rejoice in union with the Lord always! I will say it again: rejoice! Let everyone see how reasonable and gentle you are. The Lord is near! Don't worry about anything; on the contrary, make your requests known to God by prayer and petition, with thanksgiving. Then God's shalom, passing all understanding, will keep your hearts and minds safe in union with the Messiah Yeshua. In conclusion, brothers, focus your thoughts on what is true, noble, righteous, pure, lovable or admirable, on some virtue or on something praiseworthy. Keep doing what you have learned and received from me, what you have heard and seen me doing; then the God who gives shalom will be with you (Philippians 4:4–9 CJB).

About Robert Stearns

EAGLES' WINGS

Eagles' Wings is an international relational network of believers, churches, and ministries committed to the lifestyle of biblical spirituality through a lifestyle of worship and prayer, the unity of the Body of Christ, and the restoration of Israel.

Eagles' Wings is comprised of a full-time staff of 60, under the leadership of an Advisory Board with Robert Stearns serving as Executive Director. Eagles' Wings has ministered in over 30 nations, and maintains active, ongoing ministry in Honduras and Israel.

P.O. Box 450
Clarence, NY 14031
Tel: 716.759.1058
Fax: 716.759.0731

Visit our Websites:

www.eagleswings.to
www.daytopray.com
www.kairos.org

About Chuck D. Pierce

Glory of Zion International Ministries

Dr. Chuck D. Pierce has been used by God to intercede and mobilize prayer for local churches, cities, and nations throughout the world. He is an ordained minister and serves as **President of Glory of Zion International Ministries in Denton, Texas**. This ministry helps the Body of Christ understand the times and seasons, and facilitates the vision of other apostolic ministries worldwide.

Chuck also serves as **President of Global Spheres, Inc.,** an apostolic ministry for apostolic, prophetic, and intercessory leaders. He works closely with Peter and Doris Wagner in this ministry.

He is the author of many books, including:

Interpreting the Times,
Redeeming the Time, and
God's Unfolding Battle Plan

P.O. Box 1601
Denton, TX 76202
info@gloryofzion.org
www.gloryofzion.org
Tel: (940) 382-7231
Fax: (940) 565-9264

About Larry Kreider

RESOURCES FROM DOVE
CHRISTIAN FELLOWSHIP INTERNATIONAL (DCFI)

- Church Planting and Leadership Training (Live or video school with Larry Kreider and others). For a complete list of classes and venues, visit www.dcfi.org.

- School of Global Transformation. For details, visit www.dcfi.org.

- Pastors, host a seminar at your church! For more information about DCFI seminars:

Call: 800-848-5892
Email: seminars@dcfi.org

Contact Larry Kreider

Larry Kreider, International Director, DOVE Christian Fellowship International

11 Toll Gate Road
Lititz, PA 17543
Tel: 717.627.1996
Fax: 717.627.4004
www.dcfi.org
LarryK@dcfi.org

Other Books by Larry Kreider

21 Tests of Effective Leadership

Authentic Spiritual Mentoring

Biblical Foundations for Your Life two-book series:
Discovering the Basic Truths of Christianity and *Building Your Life on the Basic Truths of Christianity*

Building Your Personal House of Prayer

Growing the Fruit of the Spirit

Hearing God 30 Different Ways

Helping You Build Cell Churches Manual
compiled by Brian Sauder and Larry Kreider

House Church Networks

House to House

Speak Lord, I'm Listening

Starting a House Church

The Cry for Spiritual Fathers & Mothers

The Biblical Role of Elders in Today's Church